THE WASHINGTON PAPERS
Volume IV

41: Oil and Middle East Security

David Lynn Price

THE CENTER FOR STRATEGIC AND INTERNATIONAL STUDIES
Georgetown University, Washington, D.C.

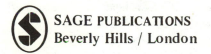

SAGE PUBLICATIONS
Beverly Hills / London

For information address:

SAGE PUBLICATIONS, INC.
275 South Beverly Drive
Beverly Hills, California 90212

SAGE PUBLICATIONS LTD
St George's House / 44 Hatton Garden
London EC1N 8ER

International Standard Book Number 0-8039-0791-5

Library of Congress Catalog Card No. 76-54450

SECOND PRINTING

*When citing a Washington Paper, please use the proper form. Remember to cite
the series title and include the paper number. One of the two following formats
can be adapted (depending on the style manual used):*

(1) HASSNER, P. (1973) "Europe in the Age of Negotiation." The Washington
Papers, I, 8. Beverly Hills and London: Sage Pubns.

OR

(2) Hassner, Pierre. 1973. *Europe in the Age of Negotiation.* The Washington
Papers, vol. 1, no. 8. Beverly Hills and London: Sage Publications.

CONTENTS

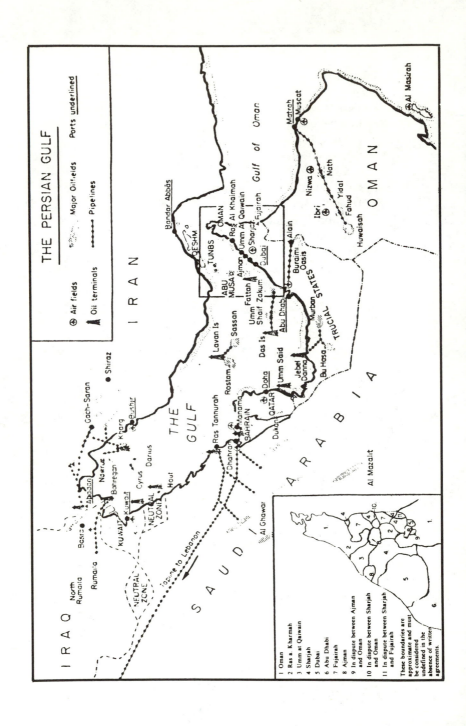

I. INTRODUCTION

A s the last quarter of the twentieth century opens, new forces are changing the world's economic order. As the economic center of gravity shifts, conventional, Western-designed political and military alignments are being reshaped. October 1973 saw Arab oil-producing states impose economic sanctions for political ends, and the oil embargo created a fundamental change in the international political system. Most of the major oil producers are in the Gulf states, and until 1973 Western policies toward the region were mainly motivated by morality, tradition, and sentiment. To a large extent this was the British view; the United States operated on a more rarefied level and for objectives rooted in American independence: namely physical security from attacks, the cultivation of conditions in which the United States could survive and prosper, and the propagation of American political ideals. Since October 1973, these policies have become more dynamic, and the Western (Bundy, 1975) and Japanese interests in the Gulf are commercial, political, and strategic.

II. WESTERN INTERESTS

Commercial Interests

No fuel is as versatile or as cheap to produce as oil, and the Gulf states have most of it. Currently these states hold 55.5 percent of the world's total proven reserves; the United States has 5.6 percent. In 1975, the United States provided 15.3 percent of the world's oil production; the Gulf producers—Iran, Iraq, Kuwait, Qatar, Saudi Arabia, Oman, and the United Arab Emirates (UAE)—managed 35.9 percent. The Western industrialized countries and Japan export no oil to the Middle East, but they imported over 1,000 million tons from the Gulf states in 1975 and will continue to do so. Japan is especially vulnerable to an oil embargo as it gets 80 percent of its total oil imports from the Middle East. Until 1973, Japan had done very little to establish relations with the Arab world. Since the embargo Japan has sent its prime minister on a visit to 16 Arab countries to consolidate Japanese-Arab friendship, and in 1976 there were two divisions in the Japanese Ministry of Foreign Affairs dealing with Arab relations, employing 38 specialists in Arabic.

The embargo compelled former President Nixon to revise completely the U.S. national energy policy, and the industrialized countries combined to form an 18-nation International Energy Agency. The ability of consumer countries to ration and stockpile supplies and to search for alternative sources cushioned them briefly from the effects of the embargo. Local fields such as Alaska and the North Sea will supplement but not replace the traditional sources because of the cost or the short life of both. In the Energy Act of December 1975, the U.S. congress required the U.S. government to buy about 500 million barrels of oil over the next seven years as a strategic petroleum reserve in the event of another oil embargo. But the scheme has run into problems over low and high sulphur crudes, storage, and distribution from the storage point to refinery. Therefore, until the United States becomes self-sufficient in energy, its principal objective in the Gulf will be to get as much oil as possible, as cheaply as possible, and for as long as possible. The era of cheap oil is over, and Western countries have no real alternative in the foreseeable future except to pay the asking price. In February 1976, the American Petroleum Institute (API) stated that increasing quantities of U.S. imported petroleum came from Arab members of OPEC rather than from traditional foreign suppliers such as Canada. The increase, according to API, was 33.3 percent and rising; and this rate of dependence makes consumers vulnerable to political instability in the producing states. This sense of vulnerability will become more acute in the future because over the next 30 years U.S. energy requirements are expected to be 50 percent higher than the amount used between 1940-1970.

But if the industrialized community needs Gulf oil, it needs Gulf markets just as much. With the exception of Iraq, the economic systems in the region are based on free enterprise. Western companies are attracted to the area by vast markets, petrodollars, favorable taxation and currency arrangements, and the pro-Western attitudes of the target countries. One British company in Saudi Arabia claimed it was encouraged to do business because of the country's political stability! The total value of trade between the United States and the Arab States is $US 3,378 million (1975). But arms sales do not normally figure in conventional trade figures; in fact in Western exports to the Gulf states, arms sales are the largest single dollar earners. The main sellers in 1974 were the United States ($4.4 billion; 54 percent of the total American arms sales); France, ($1 billion); Britain, the Soviet Union and East Europe ($360 million); and West Germany ($120 million). Compared to the United States, Moscow's share of the Middle East market is 45 percent (AID, 1975); both percentages reflect political and strategic considerations. It is this kind of trading emphasis that fuels the debate on arms sales and political influence.

Nevertheless, the colossal development programs of the Gulf states are already beginning to offer more opportunities in the civil section than in the military. Most of the states need everything from the West—from five-cent cigars to complete townships. The extent of involvement is unimaginable in the West: the Royal Saudi Air Force is completely managed by the British Aircraft Corporation (BAC) and part of the army is contracted to the Raytheon and Vinnell companies; the gas reserves of Qatar are being exploited under the guidance of Charbonnage de France Chimie (Cdf Chimie), a French government agency; and the Abu Dhabi National Oil Company (ADNOC), which is an operating arm of the government, is managed by Algerians seconded from Sonatrach.

The eight Gulf states, with a population of about 55 million, have only one resource. With the exception of Iraq, all the ruling elites can remember a pre-petroleum past when living conditions were at subsistence level; to many nomadic communities life was nasty, short, and brutish. Not surprisingly, all the states are in a hurry to develop and to evolve. Then at a later stage will come the search for viable post-oil economies. Oil-producing countries are aware that they cannot possibly reach, in a short time, the technotronic sophistication of the industrialized West. So they are happy to enter into joint ventures and other trading arrangements with the West. Each side needs to buy and each has something to sell. As the interdependence of producers and consumers coalesce, the advantages for the global economic system become obvious. Arab investors are reluctant to divulge the levels of their holdings outside the region; but they bank in Europe, buy European and American property, and invest in Eurocurrency via their own agencies, such as the Kuwait Investment Company. Iran has loaned money to Britain and Saudi loans have been made to France and the Canadian provinces. Major banks such as Chase Manhattan, First National City, or Morgan Guaranty initiate investment and offer advice to petro-dollar clients. Increasingly, Arabs and Iranian bankers are combining their capital with Western technology in such joint ventures as Swiss pharmaceuticals and Brazilian investment companies. Locked together in this way, consumers and producers have a fundamental interest in maintaining a climate favorable to the free circulation of money, which underpins the Western economic system. Periodically this interest is subjected to considerable strain; in 1975-1976, sterling underwent an alarming depreciation and severely tested the good will of Arab holders of sterling. To withdraw or convert those reserves would thoroughly discredit sterling and contribute to a world recession. Fortunately, Gulf financial ministers understand that they would also suffer in that situation.

Another danger of such intricate interdependence is that the enthusiasm of both sides can overheat the system. Between 1971 and mid-1975, Iran's civil and military development program knew no apparent limits. With hindsight it seemed as if the Shah's strategic ambitions were far in excess of (a) what he could afford and (b) the technical competence of the Iranian armed forces. In addition, a world recession and a depressed oil-price market aggravated Iran's cash flow problem so that by late 1975 and early 1976, Iran was borrowing money from the international agencies. The pace and scope of Iranian development created its own momentum, which was assisted by unplanned competitive Western sales. The moral is that you can oversell to your customer, yet to maintain goodwill that customer will continue to buy merchandise he can neither pay for nor use. In the long term, the system breaks down; and in the case of Iran it could provoke unsteadying domestic problems.

Commercial relations between the Gulf states and the West are strong and are continually evolving. But they are also anarchic; there is fierce, unrelenting competition between American, British, Japanese, French, and West German companies for Gulf markets. This kind of economic nationalism weakens any Western profession of political alliance or understanding. It often puzzles Gulf ministers to be assured, on the one hand, of Anglo-American agreement for a defense arrangement, while on the other hand, the companies involved in implementing the terms of the arrangement ruthlessly compete with each other, often with the support of the British and American governments.

There is no easy solution. Free enterprise favors the activities of U.S. firms whose goods and reputation are generally more attractive than those of rivals. But the magnitude of deals now being made in the Gulf and the critical economic and political factors involved require that Western governments become more directly involved in these deals. One method is for national governments to aid companies overseas in negotiating collectively with the target countries (Nakhleh, 1975). The Gulf states are setting an example by tentatively working toward some kind of regional economic cooperation but at governmental level. In the Gulf area, the state owns most of the wealth and the semi-industrial infrastructure that goes with it. The government is usually the largest employer; in every Gulf state, 75-80 percent of the labor force is in the public sector. Consequently, the ruling family in each state is the largest single economic unit—a Western term for this kind of economic philosophy is *étatisme* (statism). This economic system is resilient; it will continue, and it reinforces the needs for Western governments to try and bring some coordination into the activities of Western companies in the Gulf. One example is Britain's trade agreement with Saudi Arabia (a joint commission) and Qatar (a memorandum of understanding).

Political Factors

Western interest in the Gulf is assured until the end of the century. Moreover, this interest reassures the Gulf states. The majority of the states are pro-Western and this disposition makes it easier for Western countries to shape their foreign policies; Western and regional interests are best served by stability. Only in this condition can the developing states evolve. Change itself creates enormous problems for these states, so the desire for gradual and controlled change is generally consistent with Western policies. All the Gulf states recognize that stability in the Gulf means not rocking the boat. Since the British military withdrawal (1968-1971), the states of the lower Gulf have had to look to each other. They all have heroic programs that are creating socioeconomic revolutions in their systems; they therefore have common problems, and planners in the UAE are consulting with their counterparts in Qatar, Bahrain, or Kuwait. The British legacy is the spirit and skeleton of federalism, a desire to encourage the habit of cooperation; and it is beginning to work.

Britain's historical involvement in the area, nefarious to some, has left a vast fund of goodwill and locally adapted political machinery. It is almost an accident that Britain finds itself in this situation. When Britain first became involved in Gulf affairs (reluctantly) in the early nineteenth century, the aims were to prevent piracy and arms smuggling in order to leave the sea routes free for British shipping. It was only at a later stage that Britain became involved in settling shore disputes, and only then at the request of local rulers. Just as all ships benefited from the eradication of piracy, so most of the Western industrialized community has been able to enjoy the goodwill bequeathed by the British role. Arabs, Iranians, Europeans, and Americans told the author that "the British did a good job." The Arab-Israeli dispute, a nonaligned nations conference, or an OPEC* meeting sometimes distorts the pro-Western tilt of the Gulf states, but in the East-West ideological conflict, the states are emphatically in the Western community.

*OPEC: Organization of Petroleum Exporting Countries

The profound American commitment to democracy is unshakeable, and to many U.S. administrators, the traditional systems of Gulf states may appear unattractive. But the West's need for oil, markets, and friends creates diplomatic ambiguities that are facts of life. In addition, these systems are indigenous to the area and no adequate alternative has yet been devised. Periodically, dynastic changes test the traditional system and the consumer-producer relationship. With the exceptions of Iraq and the PDRY*, the pattern of succession has been favorable to the West. In some instances—Iran, Abu Dhabi, and Oman—the American and British involvement in assisting the succession was skillful and timely. It seems unlikely that in the future the West will be able to manipulate national leaderships in the Gulf as it did in the past. The political elites of the Gulf states are creating nationalism and are playing increasing roles in managing their own states. They need technical advice certainly but not political advice; in day-to-day matters they consult with each other. An Arab minister said that "foreign policies are made at airports"; habit and communications are lessening the need for Anglo-American political advice. Western insensitivity, exemplified in Dr. Kissinger's widely publicized interview in Business Week (Kissinger, 1975), may have the desired effect in the short term, but in the long term it will lead to irritation and ill-feeling.

Strategic Issues

A degree of stability ensures the continuation of oil supplies and the peaceful evolution of Gulf states; in strategic terms this means denying the area to Soviet influence. Moscow's interests are generally best served by controlled tensions. After the British military withdrawal in 1971, fears were expressed that a power vacuum would exist in the area that would allow the Soviet Union to penetrate the Gulf. This did not happen, although between 1971 and 1976 enough happened to offer the Soviet

*Peoples' Democratic Republic of Yemen

Union several opportunities: the British military withdrawal, Moscow's friendship treaty with Iraq, seizure of the Tumbs and Abu Musa islands, changes of succession, a Soviet-aided insurgency in Dhofar, the Arab-Israeli dispute, and difficulties in Arab-Iranian relations.

Happily for the West, the Arab states—with the momentary exception of Iraq and PDRY—are viscerally anticommunist. Moreover the Shah, disturbed by the closure of a British chapter in the Gulf, was determined to open an Iranian one. Detente in Europe in the early 1970s did not reassure the Shah. On the contrary, it was his view that Moscow had been encouraged to seek a hunting license elsewhere. Iran's defense program has worried some Arab states but it has worried Soviet planners even more. In 1945-1946, Soviet forces invaded Iran but were forced to withdraw by the intervention of the Allied Powers. Since then Moscow's position in the Gulf has remained weak. Briefly it found a conduit to export subversion via Baghdad and Aden. But Iraq's Friendship Treaty did not bind it immutably, and in December 1975, the Sultan of Oman announced the victory of his forces over the Popular Front for the Liberation of Oman (PFLO).

As long as the Soviet Union's room for maneuver remains limited, the strategic advantage will lie with the West. Moscow's Indian Ocean policy is still evolving, and currently Soviet naval forces are much weaker than the combined strength of the West's naval deployment. The anti-Western opposition of littoral states and domestic pressures in the West to cut defense budgets have provided a potential balance favorable to the Soviet Union. But in April 1976, the People's Republic of China and India agreed to resume diplomatic relations, and this must be considered a serious setback to Soviet influence in Asia and the Indian Ocean.

At the head of the Gulf, Iran and Iraq signed an accord in March 1975 that effectively ended Iraq's Kurdish war. This lessened Iraq's dependence on Soviet arms, and in June that year Moscow temporarily suspended its supplies to Iraq as that country turned to the West for aid and technical assistance. For the moment there seems no realistic possibility for the Soviet Union of recovering the ground it has lost. The most volatile issue in the Middle East is Lebanon, which does not really impinge on the Gulf militarily. Fortunately for the West, and for some of the regional states, the most significant strategic development is Iranian naval policy. Approximately 200 tankers a day pass through the Straits of Hormuz bound for Europe and Japan; the Arab states of the Gulf have an interest in safeguarding the sea lanes, but Iran's need is greater than theirs because of its population, size, and vast dependence on regular oil revenues. Iran has no access to pipelines, and it needs uninterrupted sea routes; these fundamental material needs are supported by the Shah's political will to extend his navy's capabilities to the Gulf, the Sea of Oman, and the northern section of the Indian Ocean. Work has begun on a naval base at Chah Behar in the Sea of Oman; in 1973, troops of the Imperial Iranian Task Force were sent to Oman to assist the Sultan's Armed Forces (SAF) in the counter-insurgency in Dhofar; and Iran has twice tried to persuade the Arab states of the Gulf to discuss regional security arrangements. There are Western critics of the Iranian defense program but the local and Western interest is directly served by Iran's naval strategy. The Iranian navy dominates the Gulf; there is no serious competition, and by the mid-1980s the Shah expects Iran to be a major Indian Ocean naval power. While Iran is building to that level, it has discouraged a precipitate withdrawal by Western navies from the Indian Ocean.

III. DESTABILIZING DOMESTIC FACTORS

Dynastic and Tribal Challenges

One view of the Gulf asserts that the traditional method of succession in the area is by assassination. The argument is well-supported. Many of the current ruling families came to power because they were the most powerful; some were ambitious and well-armed usurpers, and others were established by tribal democracy. But now, because of the pace and the pressures of change in the Gulf, it is becoming increasingly difficult to recognize the hereditary problems. With the exception of the ruling coalition in Iraq, all the regional states have enjoyed an exceptional continuity of dynastic rule. Some ruling families have been in power for 200 years—such as the al-Nahayyan dynasty of Abu Dhabi—while others, like those of Saudi Arabia and Iran, emerged in the early part of this century. Common to all of them, except the Iraqi coalition, is a pre-petroleum past. Thus, although the environment has changed in a spectacular manner, some hereditary problems remain. The severity of these problems depends on the quality of tribalism. Experts on Arab society are divided over the strength of tribalism; there are those who argue that it is as tenacious as ever. But the majority view is that oil, jobs, money, and the labor movement have made tribalism academic. The old nomadic pastoral economies have been replaced, and the great tribes of Arabia and Iran are no longer the political forces they were. Westerners are the chief mourners of decaying tribalism; few Gulf citizens regret it. Most of the leaders of the principal tribes and families have adapted smoothly to change and with typical acumen have become successful merchants in the urban areas; if they have the talent, they thrive, quite often within or close to the ruling elite.

It was the tenacity of tradition that forced the deposition of Sheikh Shakhbut by Sheikh Zayed in Abu Dhabi in 1966 and that of Sultan Said of Oman in 1970. There were incontrovertible economic reasons for their removal: in Abu Dhabi, the outgoing ruler's parsimonious policies were obstructing development plans. In a way he was fortunate in being allowed to go peacefully because he had shot his way to power in 1928. His survival until 1966 and his bloodless deposition were no mean achievements, but the transfer of power in 1928 had left suspicion and uncertainty in Abu Dhabi. Sheikh Zayed is aware that a member of his own family could challenge him one day. On the whole the influence of tribal politics at national level is proportionate to the state's modernity. In the UAE and Oman, where the advantages of oil revenues have only been enjoyed for 10 years or less, that influence is politically significant. Abu Dhabi has more tribes than any of its partners in the UAE. In the eighteenth century, the foundation of Abu Dhabi was assured by an alliance between the Beni Yas, the Manasir, the al-Dhawahir, and the Awamir. The Beni Yas are the most important and they comprise some 15 smaller tribes, which include the ruling al-Nahayyan family who are dominant in the three centers of population—Abu Dhabi town, Al Ain in the Buraimi Oasis, and the Liwa in the southwestern part of the territory. This political preeminence is not peculiar to the Gulf, nor is it indicative of the state of political development. A similar kind of lineage càn be discerned in European and American circles in which certain families, by virtue of wealth and their role in producing political leaders, are praised and damned. The critics can be important; denied wealth, privileges, and access, they attract dissenters; and if they become politically organized in the Gulf, this usually prepares the way for a coup.

In the sheikhdoms of the UAE the exceptions are Ajman, Dubai, and Fujairah, because their rulers came to power peacefully and in an orderly manner (Anthony, 1975). In 1965, Sheikh Saqr of Sharjah was deposed, with British assistance, by Sheikh Khalid. The former lost the support of his brother and other branches of the family because he colluded with Egypt and Arab nationalists in attempts to obstruct British policies in South Arabia and the Gulf. When the British suggested to the family that Sheikh Saqr be removed, they agreed, but only on condition that he be assassinated. Britain demurred and selected Sheikh Khalid, who was a successful merchant in Dubai. When the coup took place, Sheikh Saqr became a dangerous and resentful exile in Cairo. In January 1972, he organized an unsuccessful counter-coup but Sheikh Khalid was killed. He was succeeded by Sheikh Sultan bin Muhammad, his younger brother—Sharjah's third ruler in 25 years. But Sheikh Saqr is still alive and in detention in Abu Dhabi, and unless he mellows or dies he will be an unsettling factor in local and federal affairs. Further up the coast, in Ras al-Khaimah, another Sheikh Saqr, this time of the ruling Qusimi family, faces the opposition of cousins and nephews who have not forgotten the fact that 30 years ago the ruler came to power at their expense. He succeeded by taking advantage of a family dispute between his father and uncle. Then, in 1948, while the legitimate ruler was absent from the Sheikhdom, Sheikh Saqr took over. In the UAE, Ras al-Khaimah has a political influence that is disproportionate to its size and lack of oil revenues. Sheikh Saqr has been steadfastly anti-British and resents the wealth and power of his UAE partners, Abu Dhabi and Dubai, despite the fact that his state enjoys financial aid from Sheikhs Zayed and Rashid.

Because of their size and the gap between states with oil and those without it, the dynastic problems of the lower Gulf states seem more critical. The al-Thani family of Qatar is the largest ruling family in the lower Gulf and it has split into three separate lines of succession. For most of this century the rivalry between these three branches has influenced Qatari society, the latest manifestation of which was the takeover in February 1972 by Sheikh Khalifah from Sheikh Ahmed, whose financial improvidence was well-known in the lower Gulf. The volatility of Qatari dynastic disputes was fueled in July 1976 when British authorities intercepted an arms consignment at London airport. The shipment, arranged by the Qatar Embassy in Washington, consisted of six boxes marked "books," and was addressed to Doha. When opened, the boxes contained 12 Ingram submachine guns and 10,000 rounds of 9mm Smith and Wesson ammunition.

In arranging dynastic successions Oman has spilled less blood than the northern sheikhdoms. During the removal of Sultan Said in 1970, a few shots were fired. He was succeeded by his son Sultan Qaboos in a change that had been long overdue; the father was ultraconservative and had refused to spend the little money he had. Consequently, in the absence of development, the insurgency in Dhofar thrived on official neglect. The accession of the new sultan brought more vigor, direction, and money to Oman's development program; and in December 1975, the sultan announced that his forces had defeated PFLO. One of the long-term issues for Oman had been the problem of succession, but in March 1976, Sultan Qaboos married a member of his uncle's family, so that at some point an heir is assured. Succession in the Gulf is not strictly by primogeniture, but at least in Oman there is a determination to continue the Al Bu Said dynasty, which has ruled Oman since 1744. As in other states, tribalism is breaking down in Oman. In this new situation the principal tribes such as the Hinawis and Ghafiris have a status equivalent to weak political parties—Republicans and Democrats, but with no teeth. Currently the more settled tribes of the coast and the mountain areas are not a political force, nor are the desert *bedu*. But the bedu still need a supreme arbiter, and having been launched into a tinned food economy, will need careful handling. In the southern

province of Dhofar, the dissolution of tribalism has been uninten-
tionally arrested by the creation of the paramilitary force, the
firqats. Originally the firqats were a kind of counter-guerrilla
force or tribal police. Each firqat consists of surrendered enemy
personnel (about 80 percent) and tribal irregulars. They operate
in their own tribal areas, and at the height of the Dhofar campaign were responsible for the protection of these areas from
insurgent activities. As poachers turned gamekeepers, the firqats
are well paid, trained, armed with modern rifles, and are the only
possible form of law and order in their area, the *jabal* (high
ground). It is the government's policy in siting water wells to
encourage a tribal intermingling but the existence of the firqats
directly contradicts that policy. Basically the program of pacifica-
tion and development envisages a gradual evolution for the jabal,
but traditional tribal enmities and rising expectations are bound
to force the pace.

   In the northern Gulf area, states have enjoyed the advantages
of oil revenues for much longer than their lower Gulf neighbors.
Consequently, dynastic disputes have lost some of their edge in
these states as oil wealth percolates down through the layers of
society. Nevertheless there are occasional pillars of conservatism
that are difficult to dislodge. In Kuwait, there is an inherent
threat to stability in a dispute among members of the ruling
al-Sabah clan: it is between the al-Salim branch and the al-Jabir
faction, which ruled Kuwait in 1915-1916 and 1921-1950. The
dispute, about whether the crown prince and heir apparent
should also be the prime minister, has some political significance
because if the National Assembly passed a vote of no-confidence
he would either be dismissed, or more likely the ruler would
dissolve the assembly, as happened in Bahrain in 1975, but for
different reasons. It is inconceivable that the ruler of Kuwait
would fire his successor, so creating a constitutional crisis. Moreover, what assembly would commit political suicide by voting a
future ruler out of office? Sheikh Jabir of the al-Salim faction
and Crown Prince Sheikh Ahmad of the al-Jabir branch has
advocated that the crown prince should remain above politics as a

symbol of nationalist unity; that he should reign but not rule. Sheikh Jabir's aim is to separate the ruler and his heir from day-to-day politics; the logical result of this campaign would be that all power would be transferred to the prime minister. Sheikh Jabir has a lot going for him because he has considerable support from the traditional conservative elements as well as the Kuwaiti merchants who insist on greater participation in national politics than they previously enjoyed.

But Sheikh Jabir is faced with stiff opposition from the crown prince and his likely successor, Sheikh Sa'ad, the Minister of Defense and the Interior, who has a great deal of support both within the ruling family and in Kuwaiti society. Sheikh Jabir is also opposed by other members of the ruling family and merchants because of his demands for Kuwait to be more active in Gulf and Arab politics. In 1974 he was strongly criticized for his opposition to the participation agreement with the oil companies, which was a factor in the assembly's rejection of the agreement. This family dispute has aggravated Kuwaiti politics since the death of Emir Abdullah al-Salim in 1965, and if the dispute becomes acute and leads to political paralysis, a family quarrel could provoke the army's intervention.

On August 29, 1976, Kuwait's National Assembly was dissolved and harsh new press laws were imposed. The immediate occasion was the Lebanese crisis; there are about 250,000 Palestinians working in Kuwait, and some of them are in key positions in the civil service, banks, and other institutions. The Syrian military intervention in Lebanon and Kuwait's negative stance on this issue infuriated the Palestinians, and this anger erupted into bomb attacks in Kuwait and a spate of press articles suggesting that Kuwait could shortly become another Beirut.

In the National Assembly, the opposition leader, Ahmad al-Khatib of the Arab Nationalist Movement (there are no officially recognized parties in Kuwait), took advantage of the Lebanese crisis to strike out at the Kuwaiti ruling elite; he was supported by an admittedly small number of National Assembly deputies. But what he had to say was very agreeable to the Palestinians and radical elements among students, professional, and labor organizations. Although the merchants liked what Dr. al-Khatib said, they preferred to continue trading in Kuwait, and that required stability. So in the last resort they cast their votes with their pocketbooks, in support of the al-Sabah family.

The National Assembly, like that of Bahrain, was hardly an ideal model of democracy but at least it was an experiment and did encourage a lively political atmosphere, and after Beirut it had the most vociferous Arab press. In practical terms, there is no doubt that the dissolution of the National Assembly will make it easier for the government to push through important social legislation on rents, housing, and inflation. There seems little immediate prospect of the Assembly being recalled, and on the face of it, Kuwait has reverted to the system of leadership that is traditional to the region.

In March 1975, King Faisal of Saudi Arabia was assassinated by a gunman whose motives seemed more psychological than political. Before the assassination the Saudi elite displayed signs of strain and division yet, surprisingly, the transition went smoothly. One certainty is that King Khalid has won the power struggle, which few observers had anticipated. Nevertheless, the ruling elite still consists of two factions. One is led by Prince Fahad, deputy premier and minister of the interior, who is supported by his brothers Sultan (minister of defense) and Salem (governor of Riyadh). This faction has reinforced its position by appointing two more brothers, Nayef and Turki, as deputies to Fahad and Sultan. The other rival group was led by (the then) Crown Prince Khalid. His main support was provided by Prince Abdullah, Commander of the National Guard, a tribal and religious force. A clash between the two factions is conceivable because dynastic and political intrigues have been aggravated by the precaution taken to safeguard the security of the state, which is being challenged by economic change. The armed forces, the frontier police, and the National Guard are run by Prince Sultan, Prince Fahad, and Prince Abdullah, respectively. Each force has its own intelligence organization and each prince runs his own private security system. Where strong personalities are involved in a struggle for power, the diffusion of various security methods under their control usually means that those systems will be used for personal and sectional motives, not national and territorial reasons. For the moment King Khalid appears to have consolidated his kingship, but he still has to be vigilant against ambitious princes, Islamic fundamentalists, and an aspiring Western-trained intelligentsia.

> We see them confronting one another like birds of prey with hooded, watchful, expressionless eyes, waiting for the enemy to make a false move to stumble, or relax his attention, in order instantly to pounce down with a shriek and tear him apart with beak and claws. . . . These chieftains always moved about with the protection of a gang of armed officers . . . and these mobsters would occupy the corridors, and the staircases, the offices and the reception rooms of the Party headquarters.

This was Professor Kedourie's description (1974) of Syria's Baathists, but it is also an accurate image of Iraq's political condition since 1958. Following the destruction of the Hashemite dynasty by the army and General Qasim, Iraq underwent four coups and two abortive revolts. In the first instance, the army overthrew the monarchy and declared a republic. The main political organization, the Baath party, was suppressed and its supporters savagely persecuted. In 1963 Baathist officers staged a successful countercoup and extracted their revenge in extreme fashion. Since then the regime in Baghdad has been preoccupied with the struggle between civilians and the military for control of the party machinery.

Unlike the other Gulf states, Iraq's rulers can claim no dynastic pedigree. They are in power as a result of violence and coercion; challenges to authority have been ruthlessly suppressed; and most rivals and opponents have been eliminated. At the moment, President Bakr and Saddam Hussein, vice-chairman of the ruling Revolutionary Command Council (RCC), seem to have removed military opposition from positions of political influence, but they still need the support of the army to stay in power.

Iraq's rulers are trying to create tradition with a mailed fist, but the Baath regime has failed to legitimize its authority over the people. Consequently, although it seems likely to remain in power, its right to rule over a fragmented society will continue to be questioned. Despite professions of ideological purity, the government is sustained by personal, professional, and sectarian factors. In essence, President Bakr's support is drawn from a geographical elite: the social roots of most of his supporters are in Takrit, a small town in the upper Tigris. All 18 members of the regional command council of the Baath party come from this area. In this manner, the Takritis dominate Iraqi politics and their continuous search for power bases leads to expediency and compromise. The ruling coalition thus faces the opposition of its supporters for reneging on the party policy and in these circumstances a coup becomes probable.

In Iran, the dynastic succession is more assured. If the Shah were to die suddenly, the contingency plan is for a Council of Regency to be established under Queen Farah until the Shah's eldest son, Prince Reza Pahlavi (born in 1960), reaches the age of 20. So the Pahlavi dynasty should continue to rule for the foreseeable future. Since the accession of the Pahlavis in 1925, Shahs of Iran have not been seriously threatened by disaffected Pahlavi claimants. But the great tribes of Iran have presented other problems; in the mid-1920s Shah Reza finally subdued the major tribes of the south. Yet the tribal *Khans* have always been present in the Iranian power elite. Tribal representation is fluid and really depends on the eminence of a particular tribe at a certain point in its history. Not surprisingly, the presence of a tribal leader within the elite has frequently alienated those tribes that were not represented. This then aggravates bitter tribal rivalries that the Shah can manipulate in order to maintain the balance of power at court. In recent years, Bakhtiyari and Qashgai Khans have both led and helped to put down rebellions; Reza Shah executed nearly a dozen Bakhtiyari Khans while his son— the present Shah—married a Bakhtiyari princess, who became a powerful queen. The Shah's land reform programs, which began in 1963, have probably destroyed forever the political power of tribal chieftains, but their influence is still considerable and could become destabilizing should they ally with the new urban-based middle class emerging in Iran.

Ironically, one of the aims of the White Revolution was to destroy the traditional order, which among other things obstructted development. But the pace of development has aroused immense expectations and has created new urban forces that will not acquiesce to the posture of deference the Shah demands. To preserve the system, the ruler may then have to look for the support of the traditional chieftains whose power he destroyed. It will be in their interests to ally with the Shah, but what price will they ask?

Territorial Disputes

Before the discovery of oil, territorial disputes remained at the level of grazing or water rights, or taxation (*Zakat*) and tribal limits. But oil and the rise of nationalism have compelled states to define precise land and sea frontiers, some of which are still being negotiated. The most combustible dispute is between Kuwait and Iraq. In 1961, General Qasim claimed Kuwait, but he was disappointed when Kuwait called in British and Arab League forces to fight off the challenge. Nevertheless, Kuwait still had to buy off Iraq's challenge to the value of U.S. $70 million. In 1973, Iraqi and Kuwaiti troops clashed at the Kuwaiti borderpost of Al-Samita. Then, Kuwait called on Saudi troops to assist its own forces. The dispute between the countries is over the Kuwait-owned islands of Bubiyan and Warbah, which hinder Iraq's access to the sea. This claim is still unresolved, and in 1975 it was the principal reason for Kuwait's reluctance to join in talks on Gulf security.

Kuwait supports any measure that increases the security of the Gulf and any method of achieving this aim *provided* all existing problems between the states have been settled [Middle East International, 1976].

Currently, there is a hopeful sign that the dispute could lose some of its combustibility because both countries are considering a deal in which Kuwait would lease the islands in return for fresh water supplied from Iraq. But Kuwait is still vulnerable to Baghdad's pressure politics; if the Iraqi coalition feels strong enough, or needs a face-saving foreign adventure, another border incident is conceivable. Since spring 1976, there have been discreet diplomatic movements between Iraq and Saudi Arabia with Kuwait acting as broker. The pan-Arab quality would suggest this diplomacy is anti-Iranian in concept, but if the suspicions among the three countries are relaxed, one may expect that the Kuwait-Iraq dispute will moderate.

In the early 1950s, Saudi Arabia, Abu Dhabi, Oman, and Britain fought a brief skirmish over the villages of the Buraimi oasis. The dispute was taken to the United Nations, where the verdict went against Saudi Arabia. The dispute—strategic, economic, and sentimental—was formally ended in 1974, when Sheikh Zayed and King Faisal signed an agreement that made territorial adjustments on both sides. Any tensions that remain are at a tribal, not a governmental, level. North and northeast of Buraimi is the territory of an Omani tribe, the 20,000-strong Beni Kaab. Leading members of this tribe are still bitter at the intrigue and turbulence provoked by the Saudis 25 years ago. Equally troublesome are the internecine murders still being committed in attempts to settle old scores between pro- and anti-Saudi supporters of the Beni Kaab. Like all blood feuds, settling old scores only opens new ones. (During conversations in Buraimi, the Wadi Sharm, and the Wadi Jizzi in 1974, the author heard numerous expressions of distrust of the Saudis and was shown what purported to be the graves and memorial stones of Beni Kaab tribesman.) The dormant fear of some Omanis is that Saudi Arabia may revive its expansionist aims and invade northern Oman, in an effort to give Saudi Arabia an Indian Ocean coastline. Under the present Saudi leadership this is not a serious prospect, but a republican Saudi Arabia could have different ideas on what would constitute territorial sovereignty.

Probably the least soluble of the territorial disputes are those between Iran and the lower Gulf states. Traditional Arab-Iranian tensions are aggravated by undecided maritime limits between Iran on the one hand, and Dubai, Umm al-Qaiwan, Ajman, Fujairah, and Ras al-Khaimah on the other. Relations with the latter are particularly contentious because of the Iranian occupation of the Tumbs islands (claimed by Ras al-Khaimah) in November 1971. Earlier, the Shah had revived a territorial claim to Bahrain because he opposed the island's inclusion in any federation. But a U.N. mission negotiated an independent status for Bahrain in 1970, which satisfied all parties. Ras-al-Khaimah's neighbor, Ajman, which lost Abu Musa to Iran in 1971, has accepted the loss. But Sheikh Saqr of Ras al-Khaimah still resents the Iranian occupation of the Tumbs; his spirited, but ineffective, resistance to the occupation made him something of a folk hero in the sheikhdom. In view of Iran's overwhelming military superiority, the sheikhdom's dissenters can do very little. Although the dispute may have a certain cartoon quality, the long-term dangers are that it feeds Arab-Iranian rivalry and makes hostages of Iranian citizens in Ras al-Khaimah. In November 1971, local Arabs attacked Iranians and damaged Iranian property.

For 10 years, Oman's dissident southern province of Dhofar was the arena for a communist-backed insurgency. Dhofar's cultural and geographical uniqueness gave the conflict a distinct territorial dimension. Had it escalated it would have become much more than that, because PFLO's strategy was regional and pan-Arab. But the government's counterinsurgency campaign succeeded in confining the guerrillas in that province. In December 1975, the Sultan of Oman announced a military victory over PFLO and by the middle of 1976 there was total military security throughout Dhofar.

At a lower level, territorial disputes have lost their edge since 1971. At the base of the Musandum peninsula there is a confusing jigsaw puzzle of sheikhdoms and enclaves that cause occasional wrangling between Ajman, Dubai, Sharjah, Fujairah, and Oman. But the disputes are so parochial and the territorial segments so small that they only possess a local nuisance value.

Qatar's ruling family has conducted a running battle with Bahrain for more than a century; the grievances date from the time when Bahrain Sheikhs occupied most of the Qatar peninsula. Dynastic and territorial claims are inextricably involved. The Bahrainis disparage Qatar's al-Thani dynasty as upstart Bedouins and hick Arabs. This assumed superiority is aggravated because the al-Khalifahs of Bahrain claim jurisdiction over people living in Zubarra on the west coast of the Qatar peninsula. The remains of the first al-Khalifah ruler of Bahrain are buried in Zubarra, the site from which the al-Khalifahs set out to conquer Bahrain in the late eighteenth century. Near the west coast of Qatar are a group of islands, the Hawar islands, over which Bahrain claims sovereignty. Each side has produced maps that exclude each other's claims. External mediation has failed to resolve these claims to Zubarra and the Hawar islands. One solution proposed is that Bahrain would be agreeable to an offer by Qatar to buy off the claim. But again, Qataris suspect that the selling price would be too high.

Haves and Have-Nots

Some of the states have oil but others are without it; those without oil are not only the poorest but also the smallest. It is characteristic of the Gulf that it has some of the world's richest states and also some of the most penurious. The problem is especially acute in the UAE, which is dominated by Abu Dhabi and Dubai. These sheikhdoms have wealth, size, and power and represent a monopoly that is resented by the less endowed sheikhdoms. But though the non-oil states may resent the political and economic weight of Abu Dhabi, Iran, Kuwait, and Saudi Arabia, they do enjoy financial assistance, formally and privately, from the oil states for aid and national development. In this manner, the yawning inequality between states is reduced and, as a result, the economic disparity is not a major security problem.

But within these states oil wealth has created serious problems. Despite their wealth, the oil states of the Gulf are still developing countries and, with the exception of Bahrain and Kuwait, they still have rudimentary infrastructures. All the regional states are ruled by principal families, and in traditional manner, the oil revenue is the personal property of the ruling family. Despite the admirable development programs of Iran, UAE, and Oman, there are domestic dissenting voices protesting that change is neither rapid nor equitable. This is less of a problem in the lower Gulf because these states started later and are smaller than those of the northern Gulf. The beauty of smallness is that there is a high per capita income and the states can distribute the wealth more widely, so that it percolates to all levels. Where inequalities exist they arise not so much from willful selectivity, but more from administrative bottlenecks or sheer isolation. But some Arab intellectuals, admittedly thinking on a pan-Arab level, have disagreed:

> The Arab effort in October was not properly and equitably shared. While some willingly sacrificed their blood . . . others simply accumulated large fortunes due to the gold that flooded their coffers. The rich got richer, whereas those who initially spilled their blood had to turn around and spill their dignity, asking for a little of the material wealth that others had acquired because of the sacrifices made by the poor [Al Tali'a, 1975].

It is this kind of thinking that also accuses Saudi Arabia of being no more than a Sudeiry corporation. To some extent the view is accurate but incomplete. Abu Dhabi's modernity is barely a decade old and it has a chronic lack of skilled managers and bureaucrats. Oman's development is even more recent—1970—and it has the major physical problems of being a large country but with only three centers of population. Oman has many remote communities that can only be reached after days by man-pack. Given the shortage of manpower, the pace of development, and the general upsurge of expectation, Oman will have difficulty in regulating the tempo of change. For example, the internal system of government, the *wilayat* system, is under pressure because of the differing caliber of the *Wali*. It is a fairly common event for a Wali to be transferred from his decaying, fly-blown fort in the interior to a coastal residence of steel and glass with a limousine at the door. The economic and cultural gap is often unbridgeable.

Where the ruling family dispenses wealth, privilege, and opportunity it is usually granted to the present elite. Those who are not members of the charmed circle are in that position either from choice or for political and economic factors. That is, they have neither contacts, talent, nor money. But these deficiencies do not stop them from complaining.

In Saudi Arabia, the spectacular development program has become the forcing house for an indigenous Western-educated group, the intelligentsia. In Saudi Arabia's traditional and theocratic society, the steady and irresistible growth of this class is bound to intensify the demand for power-sharing. To admit the cosmopolitan technocrat into the Sudeiry elite will inevitably dilute the political authority of the ruling family. Some will be absorbed because they are needed, they are conservative, and they depend on the state for employment. But the process of assimilation will never be rapid enough. The educational system is already uneven, and it is turning out a highly trained product that is under- or unemployed. The growth of this class will create a logjam in the system as one group aspires, while the entrenched elite vegetates. Ultimately the exclusion of the intelligentsia will force the emergence of a group united in its political frustration, thus preparing the way for a power struggle unless the state's security agencies move first.

The system of government in the Gulf has its critics, but it is a traditional system and no adequate alternative has yet been devised. Nonetheless, the exclusive nature of dynastic authority does encourage political ossification. This is dangerous at a time when new groups and classes are challenging the traditional patterns of politics.

In the early 1960s in Iran, several representative groups of the professional middle class had increased to such a size and made demands to a degree that seriously threatened the traditional elite system. Therefore, in January 1963 the Shah (1967) introduced his "White Revolution," which was designed to "put an end to all the social inequalities and all the factors which caused injustice, tyranny and exploitation." Apart from introducing belated economic reforms, the program had a political purpose in that it met the demands of the intelligentsia whose members had for years been campaigning for the lower classes. But as early as 1967, increased oil revenues were insufficient to fund the gigantic land reforms. The Shah still has to contend with critics who argue that less money should be spent on defense and more on agriculture. Although the program has been successful in reforming the major part of the traditional land system, it has also encouraged rising expectations among the peasantry. Too many schemes are capital—not labor—intensive, and many farmers have been driven off the land. The lack of sufficient skilled manpower has led to inefficiency, insecurity, and a peasant mistrust of urban-based officials. In short, the distribution of benefits has been uneven. Of a population of about 33 million, about 21 million live poorly, are largely illiterate, and account for less than one-sixth of private consumption. The economic opportunities are unequally distributed, so the young and the ambitious leave the land for the cities. Not everyone wants to remain a farmer. Government advisers are discouraged by rural obstinacy; some are angered by the gap between the urban elite and the peasants they instruct, while others refuse to leave the cities.

There was stiff resistance to the reforms: in June 1963 there were riots in Tehran; the Prime Minister was assassinated in January 1965; and in April 1965 the Shah escaped an assassination attempt. Currently, the results of urban drift and economic inequality created by the reforms are politically volatile. The unemployed, landless peasant existing at subsistence level in urban areas is good material for subversive propaganda; the political attitudes acquired in urban slums are corrosive and radical. Since 1971 large numbers of these casualties of the Iranian economic boom have been recruited into the ranks of urban guerrilla groups. In Iran, the inequalities in dividing the spoils of oil wealth result from the conception of economic planning. Development plans have rarely been formulated by those with any real political authority, so that Iranian economic affairs are given low priority in the Shah's own political program. The burden of arms purchases is considered by the Shah to be fundamental to his principal aim of being the leading power in the Gulf and Indian Ocean. The danger is that the budget for arms will impose cuts in welfare programs; with such a large population this would be dangerous. Equally, although the Shah's defense program has been modified since late 1975, he is still more concerned domestically with his own political security than with providing jobs, housing, and food. The price of external security could be the erosion of domestic support. Some of the idealistic members of the volunteer corps formed to implement the land reforms are already disillusioned and have begun to wonder whether the Shah's development plans are so well-founded; they have observed that prestige projects have taken precedence over greater rural welfare.

Not all members of Iran's intelligentsia have been alienated by the reform program; its sheer scope has attracted some of the best people who are prepared to work within the system (Bill, 1972). Intellectual satisfaction and self-interest have been merged in the Iranian elite; but this commitment is conditional, to some extent, on the success of the program. The professional and administrative intelligentsia—the middle class—has not committed itself, because the land reforms have been implemented according to traditional patterns. The Iranian elite has attempted to minimize the challenge to its authority by recruiting members of the middle class into the charmed circle, but the majority of that class has kept its distance; this is in spite of the fact that that elite is exceptionally talented. What the critics see is "nepotism, sycophancy and compromise" (Bill, 1972). The critical objectivity of the intelligentsia is a problem to the Shah, and since 1971 the number of political prisoners has increased and censorship is now more acute than in the 1950s. In the longterm, the Shah cannot afford to ignore the Iranian middle class, nor is it realistic to resort to police action—imprisonment, exile, or censorship. The only constructive development is for the patrimonial elite system to recognize and adapt to the new situation. The economic and social resources are now available in terms of wealth and trained manpower, but if the political will is not present, the system will fall under its own weight. Iranian history offers several examples of dynastic crises that were precipitated by the disintegration of the ruling elite when faced with new challenges. The Pahlavi dynasty is currently facing a challenge.

Throughout the region, the consequences of oil wealth and change have created a growing middle class of significant political influence, as well as a manpower shortage; education and travel have instilled political awareness, encouraged the emancipation of women, and begun the insidious breakdown of family unity. In too many instances, vast national budgets create an impression of prosperity and growth while a high percentage of the native people remain backward and deprived. Throughout the lower Gulf, the nomadic *bedu* have been launched into a consumer society, but at a cost; the shanty towns bordering the principal cities in Saudi Arabia emphasize the blatant inequalities of income and wealth. All the governments are making awesome efforts to reduce the inequalities but they will never be enough. Population growth, declining mortality, and urban drift have produced more people but less food available to feed them. In the next decade it will not be the depletion of oil resources that will be the major issue but the question of how to feed the region's growing population. In short, the politics of the 1980s in the Gulf will be largely determined by food, its quantity, and who gets it.

Natives and Immigrants

Possessing traditional systems and committed to industrialization, all the Gulf states need expatriate assistance at all levels. Throughout the region there is a large unquantifiable number of Europeans, Americans, Japanese, Iranians, Pakistanis, Baluchis, Indians, and nationals of every Arab country, including Palestinians. Defense contracts alone create their own majorities: by 1980 the U.S. Defense Department estimates that nearly 150,000 Americans will be working in the Gulf, fulfilling military and economic contracts. Kuwait's population is nearly one million, only half of which is native-born—a proportion that frightened the Kuwaitis into the realization that they could become a minority in their own country.

This kind of ratio creates political problems in the Gulf. In recent years it was most controversial in Oman, where the presence of expatriates—British, Pakistani, Indian, Egyptian, and Jordanian—in the military and civil sectors provided PFLO and its supporters with a sitting target. But Sultan Qaboos has explained that Oman has chosen to rely on expatriates for the simple reason that there are not sufficient skilled Omanis to do all the necessary jobs. Second, Sultans of Oman have called on expatriate advice and assistance for over 200 years. Oman's treaty relationship with Britain began in 1798 in order to preempt French interest in the territory. Since then British-Omani links have acquired a special relationship covering economic and political affairs. British military involvement in Oman was formalized in July 1958 in an Exchange of Letters. In it, Britain agreed, at Oman's request, to provide regular officers on secondment from the British Army, to provide training facilities for Oman's armed forces, and to advise on training and other matters. Currently some 500 British officers and N.C.O.s are seconded or individually contracted to SAF and other sections of the Sultan's government. Now that the war in Dhofar is over and as the level and numbers of trained Omanis increase, expatriate involvement will diminish.

Foreign experts in the military sector are one category, but two other types attract attention in the Gulf: the skilled expatriate—who is well paid and is either close to the ruling elite or an integral member of the new middle class in the area, and the immigrant laborer—the hewer of wood and drawer of water.

The quality of expatriate advisers is variable. There are carpet-baggers whose advice is more costly than constructive, and there are honest men whose altruism is close to saintliness. Some advisers live in a style of blatant opulence and privilege that becomes a natural target for resentment. Successful foreign merchants, as a rule, ally closely with the ruling family. Usually they have industry, wealth, and privileged access, and these qualities arouse the enmity of the less talented native. This is especially acute if the plaintiff is a member of a more distant branch of the ruling family. As in industrialized countries, there are common grievances over privileges and deprivation among natives and immigrants.

The demographic patterns of the Gulf states are now beginning to be controlled. Since 1968, non-Kuwaitis have been encouraged to resign and retire—for a financial consideration—from official and administrative posts to make way for the increasing number of trained Kuwaitis. Only the university and the judiciary are exempt from employing expatriates. Since February 1976, the immigration authorities in the UAE have begun to impose visa restrictions in the wake of the influx of refugees from the Lebanese civil war; at present no Palestinians are permitted to settle in Oman and any who enter Oman for business reasons are carefully screened.

Lower down the economic scale, the immigrant laborer predictably earns less; because of the Gulf's construction boom, there is a growing class whose members are employed as domestic servants, port laborers, waiters, porters, messengers, street sweepers, guards, and maintenance men in offices.

The average daily rate in 1976 for this class was U.S. $3 to U.S. $4. This is much less than a local Arab of Bedouin origin can earn in the oil industry. Moreover the unskilled immigrant is discriminated against because he is in competition with native-born labor. These subsistence-level immigrants are usually Baluchis, Keralans, Pathans, Yemenis, and Omanis. Despite the dismal level and standards these immigrants endure, they work in the Gulf because they need the jobs and the money, most of which is sent home. At this level there is no evidence of political consciousness or labor organization, but tensions do exist within this amorphous proletariat. Few of them have any rights; they are badly paid and poorly housed; and there are ethnic and sectarian grievances between all groups—Iranians and Arabs, Pakistanis and Indians, and between the Baluchis and most other groups. In 1968 in Dubai, Iranians and Baluchis went on strike over poor working conditions.

If radical ideologies take root, they will probably do so between the indigenous and immigrant communities. There are grievances to be exploited for political ends. So far, the regional states have generally resorted to police action—expulsion—to settle complaints. But that cannot continue indefinitely, because although the immigrant class structures have been formed outside the system, they are of critical importance for the development strategies of all the states:

> Were the Egyptians to be removed many of the school systems would have to close; were the Palestinians to be forced to leave the media would cease to function; were the British, Jordanian, Pakistanis, Baluchi, Yemeni, and Omani soldiers to be expelled, the defence and internal security network would collapse; were the Iranians, Baluchis, and Pathans who make up the bulk of the labor force to be sent back to their homelands, progress on such vital development projects under way, as the building of roads, ports, irrigation schemes, housing projects, schools and medical clinics would all come to an abrupt halt [Anthony, 1975].

Recent additions to the labor forces include South Koreans and Filipinos. In the *suqs* of the Gulf, the human variegation is most colorfully apparent in the Pakistani, Iranian, or Indian stores that enjoy a faithful, largely ethnic, clientele.

In the lower Gulf, there is another, more subtle problem. In Oman, since the accession of Sultan Qaboos in 1970, large numbers of Omanis who had emigrated have returned to Oman. Among them are the Zanzibari Omanis. These are highly educated Arabs of Omani origin who had emigrated to Zanzibar in the nineteenth and twentieth centuries. Following the revolution in Zanzibar in 1964 they were invited to return to Oman by Sultan Sa'id. Resentment and envy exists between these gifted returnees, some of whom do not speak Arabic, and the indigenous Omanis who, having served their time in the bad old days, now see their expectations disappointed. This division also conditions attitudes toward the Sultan; he is popular with the overwhelming majority of Omanis, but cosmopolitan returnees of broader culture are more objective.

Islam and Change

In 1976, the museums and universities of Western Europe were exposed to a cultural exhibition, the Festival of Islam. For Britain it was the first such cultural manifestation since 1910, and for thousands of Europeans it became a memorable intellectual experience. For the majority the festival was little more than an informational exercise but some discerning viewers came away troubled. They saw the fragility, texture, and imagination of Islamic art and the richness of Islamic society. But the traditional Muslim reservoirs are facing socially disruptive economic changes and color television.

All the Gulf countries are Islamic states in which the Koran is the basis for society and its laws. As the Prophet, Mohammed assumed the leadership of a religious group and became its military and political leader. This pattern has survived until the present day and has come to be considered as the ideal form of an Islamic state. It exists in its present form in Saudi Arabia. Faced with change, Islamic tradition has been unexpectedly elastic; the *sharia* (Koranic law) has been applied to Western trade and economy and in some cases is no more than a direct translation of foreign laws. Inevitably this kind of compromise does mean a degree of secularization that disturbs the ultraconservative Islamic fundamentalists. But this inevitable dilution is less of a political problem than the free thinking that such a process provokes. As in Renaissance Europe, doubts and criticisms increase—the question is who shall judge the judges? In time the entire traditional political system is questioned. If the doubts are resolved peacefully, a model is the Bahrain political system; but this experiment ended abruptly in 1975 when the National Assembly was dissolved. Modern Islamic scholars now exercise self-criticism and are prepared to repudiate the teaching of the past on fatalism, the inferiority of women, and blind obedience to authority. The exploitation of the peasantry and the *bedu* by the rich and privileged must no longer be tolerated; otherwise the inertia of Islam and the doctrinaire *ulama* will make recruits for communism.

During the 1960s the Shah's land reforms were violently resisted by Shiite religious leaders, and even in June 1975, there were confessional riots in Qum, a shrine city. The riots were swiftly contained and the riot leaders were arrested. But the demonstrators had been organized to commemorate the 1963 agrarian riots. The Qum demonstration received support from the religious leader, Ayatollah Khomeini, exiled in Iraq, who had issued an anniversary statement. Since 1971, urban terrorist groups in Iran have included an element that the security authorities call "Islamic-Marxists"; one of its manifestations has been the National Liberation Movement (NLM), which has committed bank raids, kidnappings, and sabotage, though it has, until now, refrained from methods of selective assassination. While proclaiming its fidelity to the Iranian constitution, the NLM's first political demand (in 1971) was parliamentary representation for five religious leaders. In May 1975, two U.S. advisers were killed by gunmen who claimed to be members of the Crusaders of the Iranian Nation; the group was previously unknown and it now seems probable that the gunmen were Islamic-Marxists. In August, the authorities announced a major success in arresting seven leading terrorists, some of whom had been involved in the May killings. Items found in the terrorists possession included 10 small arms, 700 rounds of ammunition, 25 hand grenades, five bombs, a large quantity of explosives, and incendiary equipment. The terrorists had operated from a number of safe houses in the most expensive parts of Tehran. Nearly all those arrested were students, and the ringleaders were Muslim extremists.

In itself, dissent in the Gulf states is not sufficiently organized to threaten seriously the national security of those states. But dissidents do become serious when they coalesce with the grievances of deprivation and sectional interests. In Iran the connection between sectarian unrest and declining oil exports may not be immediately apparent. In March 1976, the Iranian general budget was announced; expenditure was set at U.S. $29.7 billion but the revenues were U.S. $27.6 billion, a deficit of U.S. $2.1 billion. Less money in the system means that someone has to go without; those groups cut off from the majority values will complain, and in this manner grievances escalate, creating anti-Pahlavi recruits for Iran's conservative theocrats.

Propagandists of the Arab-Israeli dispute frequently attempt to disarm criticism by drawing attention to the sectarian divisions of Christendom. But this is glass-house behavior; the esoteric schools of Islam have differed enough to cause serious political crises. When complicated by nationalism these disputes lead to the kind of tense competition between Riyadh and Cairo for the leadership of Islam that assisted in Nasser's death. Throughout Islam and the Middle East, traditionalists and reformers have clashed. President Nasser, in the early years of his rule, arrested and executed the leaders of the ultraconservative Muslim Brotherhood. Reformers are not always motivated by scholastic purity; a theocracy like Saudi Arabia is sensitive to a Khaddafi-style Islamic revival.

In the early part of the seventh century, the Ibadhi Muslims, a conservative sect, distanced themselves from orthodox Islam following a doctrinal dispute. After the death of Mohammed, the Ibadhis chose their own system of leadership by electing an *Imam* (one who leads) by popular consensus. This brought the Ibadhi Imams into conflict with the Khalifate, and the sinews of secular-temporal rivalry are discernible in Oman even today. In 1957 an Imamate revolt with Saudi support erupted in the interior of Oman, led by Imam Ghalib; but in 1959, with British military assistance, it was defeated. For two years the revolt seriously threatened the stability of northern Oman as Ghalib, his brother Talib, and Suleiman bin Himyar claimed control over the religious capital of Nizwa and the Jebel Akhdar (Green Mountain). The political potential of the Imam's rebellion lay in the support he received from Suleiman's tribe, the Ghafiri, and the Sheikh Salih of the Hinawi. Between them, these four controlled most of the interior of Oman.

Modern Omanis consider the Ibadhi traditionalists as bigoted, doctrinal killjoys, but in favorable circumstances they can be dangerous. In November 1972, a PFLOAG (later PFLO) defector spotted a senior member of the movement, Muhammed bin Talib, in Muttrah. This alerted security forces, and after six weeks surveillance, the government launched Operation Jason on December 23, 1972, to destroy the subversive network. The operation was completed in five days and 90 people were rounded up. Those observers who had argued that the Imamate was a dead issue were surprised to learn that the majority of those rounded up during the dragnet were Ibadhi Omanis, some being the sons of wealthy sheikhs and merchants. A number of the surviving ring-leaders of the Imamate revolt of the 1950s are known to have had contact with the PFLO, although it is unlikely there was a meeting of minds between the groups.

On the whole, in the latter part of the twentieth century, while Islam still determines the nature of Gulf society, the political power of the Imams and Muftis may have weakened, but their influence is still considerable.

In 20 years, Bahrain has experienced five serious riots and demonstrations; some have been sectarian, between the state's Sunni and Shia Muslims. Because of this division, the ruler of Bahrain has to pay more attention to the views of the religious leaders than rulers of other states where secularization has followed oil wealth. The ruling family, Al Khalifah, and the leading merchant families are Sunni, while the majority of the population is believed to be Shia—the laboring classes that live in comparative penury. This religious-economic cleavage does present serious problems on the political front for Bahrain. In the 1960s, influential Shias supported the radical programs of the Arab Nationalist Movement (ANM), Baathists, and PFLOAG; some of them campaigned successfully as independents for the National Assembly in 1973 and are generally considered to be progressives. The cohesion and determination of the Shia radicals has unnerved the ruling family; despite the creation of the National Assembly— which was dissolved in 1975—there is no real indication by the al-Khalifah of granting Bahrain's proletariat any political participation. Currently, religious differences and political demands have become inextricably involved in Bahrain. Unless the Assembly is recalled, Bahrain will face a constitutional crisis: the ruling family may decide to change the system of entry to the Assembly (that is, some will be elected and some will be nominated), and when that happens a political experiment in the Gulf will have ended. Some Western observers have expressed fears that Bahrain could well become the Gulf's first communist state.

The Armed Forces

The late Sultan Said of Oman said that "all revolutions in the Arab world are led by colonels . . . I am having no Arab colonels in my army" (Smiley and Kemp, 1975). There was some point to his wariness because he himself survived an assassination attempt—by army officers—in 1966. But none of the Gulf rulers can afford to be without armed forces. No matter how benevolent and imaginative a ruler may be, his position critically depends on his relationship with the army. Some of the Gulf's dynasties came into being as a result of the exercise of military strength: Ibn Saud as a military leader conquered Saudi Arabia by sword; the founder of the Pahlavi dynasty in Iran was an officer in the Persian Cossack Brigade; in 1968, Brigadier Qasim and his "Free Officers" destroyed Iraq's Hashemite dynasty; and in 1969, air force mutineers in Dhahran failed to depose the Saudi ruling family.

All the armies of developing countries have officers who are personally ambitious, politically impatient, or who could be professionally alienated by weak civilian leadership. In the Gulf, a republican Saudi Arabia is conceivable, and the emergence of an Arab Cromwell even more so. While the armed forces are fighting wars there is little time for political intrigue. But in the absence of hostilities many regiments have to be either stood down, kept busy, or demobilized. Armies are kept best employed when fighting, but inactivity creates indolence or restlessness. In 1967, thousands of Yemenis streamed out of South Yemen (now the People's Democratic Republic of Yemen, PDRY) into North Yemen and Saudi Arabia. King Faisal organized some of the Yemeni exiles into two regiments that were meant to be a kind of long-range deep penetration force. Initially, these forces were well paid for good results, but the King's interests shifted elsewhere and although the exile armies were still paid, in the long run, the armies became used to being paid, but not for fighting.

The Western-inspired debate on arms control or arms embargo provokes little interest in the Gulf. International restraints are unlikely to deter a defense minister or ruler, imbued with the desire and the money, from getting what he needs for his arsenal. Consequently, there is an artificiality in Western arguments about the role of national arms purchases and their effect on Gulf security.

All the states have standing armies, most of which are indulged by the rulers in that the armed forces receive the largest portion of the national budget. For example, since 1970, Iran's military budget has risen 500 percent, Iraq's by 200 percent, and Saudi Arabia's by 700 percent. Few of the Gulf states are threatened with military invasion except for Kuwait and Iran. Iranian defense planners work on the basis that the Iraqi forces are keyed up for a rush toward the Iranian frontiers.

Throughout the Gulf, boredom is a threat to stability. Many people in the Gulf—indigenous and expatriate—have little to do and armies are not immune to this condition; they must preserve the security of the ruling family in the first place, maintain national security, and defend the frontiers. It is a popular joke that the armies are mainly cosmetic, but some have seen active service. Iraq and Saudi Arabia have dispatched units to the

Arab-Israeli theater, where admittedly they appeared without distinction. Iraqi forces—until 1975—have been fighting a Kurdish insurgency for nearly a decade; in Oman the SAF recently (December 1975) won a 10-year war in Dhofar. SAF's campaign has been assisted since 1973 by the presence of about 3,000 troops of the Imperial Iranian Task Force (IITF). It is probable that about 15,000-18,000 troops have been rotated in Dhofar in the last three years. Because of their role in shaping state institutions, the armies become major forces for nationalism. An army has the manpower, the equipment, and the bureaucracy to stitch together town and country. Army units build roads, houses, and dig wells; they transport the population to schools, hospitals, and training centers. In many cases, for example Oman, after the ruling family, the army is the largest employer and leading dispenser of contracts.

Despite their role in nation building, the armed forces are still regarded as the preserve of the ruling family. In some cases—Saudi Arabia—the senior commanders are members of the ruling family; in other instances, the rulers provide for themselves and the personal security of their families by creating a palace guard. This separation has presented problems in that some commanders have been attracted by palace politics, which has led them to be derelict in their duties; often an elite palace guard causes friction by assuming a superiority over other units, especially if the latter have well-earned battle honors. Most of the Gulf armies have sizable *beduin* or peasant contingents, which are generally fanatically loyal to the commander-in-chief, namely the ruler. But some senior commanders who prefer the court to the barracks seek and receive most of the favors. Inevitably, those who are profligate are bailed out by their friends at court, much to the resentment and envy of the rank-and-file. In the past this kind of socioeconomic grievance has provoked mutinies, and not only in the Arab world, that have been contained by timely offers of cash and promotion. Not surprisingly, some commanders will continue to prefer the attractions of the court to the lethal realities of the battlefield.

Since 1971, there has been keen debate over the disparity of the Abu Dhabi Defense Force (ADDF) and the much smaller Union Defense Force (UDF). The smaller states had expressed their uneasiness at the imbalance. In 1975, Jordan, Saudi Arabia, and Kuwait advised on the merger of the forces. The proposals for a merger were considered in December of that year at a meeting of the UAE's Supreme Council; the prospects then looked bleak as the meeting was adjourned because the rulers asked for more time to study the proposals. But in May 1976, the ADDF was merged with the federal force. Some of the rulers such as those of Ras-al-Khaimah and Fujeirah were reluctant to prune their palace guards, but Sheikh Zayed and the UDF's Jordanian chief-of-staff, General Awwad Khaldi, seem determined to proceed with the merger. At this early stage, the main problems are getting across the idea of cooperation and standardizing military equipment because the forces of Abu Dhabi, Dubai, and Ras-al-Khaimah possess three different types of rifle. At present the total strength of the UAE's forces—all arms—is 21,400.

Logically, the regional armies have evolved from the picturesque tribal *askars* carrying bolt-action fowling pieces to trained and disciplined regiments armed with modern weaponry. By the nature of things their training conditions them to take a different view of society than their civilian partners. In the Northern Gulf—Iraq and Iran—there is a familiar pattern of army intervention in politics. To some extent the interventions were carried out by officers who were imbued with European concepts of discipline and efficiency that they believed would reform their traditional societies. These foreign concepts were certainly a factor in Ottoman politics in the early part of the twentieth century. If anything, the influence of European ideas on indigenous armies has actually increased. Officers and officials close to the army are still isolated by their Western ideas from the societies they are meant to serve. The presence of expatriates in the regional forces, either as advisors or serving officers, is really irrelevant to these concepts because for the foreseeable future, the forces will still be trained to European or Anglo-American programs.

In Saudi Arabia, the most serious challenge to the regime was the abortive coup of September 1969. The conspiring group included several young air force officers, including the commander of the Mecca region as well as several Saudi defense attachés abroad. The signs are that the military establishment will be increased with more men and more sophisticated equipment, and it would seem likely that the growth of new centers of opposition in the army and air force cannot be discounted.

For traditional and technological reasons, there are innumerable expatriate defense advisers in the region and some actually serve in the colors as in the UAE and Oman. In these countries, nearly all the key positions are held by expatriate officers, usually British or Jordanian. Some observers argue that the Arabization of the armed forces will in the long term render them politically vulnerable to intrigue and factionalism, especially as the Arab officer cadre works its way through the system. The presence of expatriate advisers insulates the indigenous forces against political influence, and many rulers prefer to retain the expatriate advisers for that reason. But the pressures of Arabization are considerable and irresistible and rulers have to accommodate such pressures. When they do so, the indications are that it will be an expatriate Arab who will be appointed. On March 1, 1976, a Jordanian, Major-General Awwad M. Khaldi, was appointed the first chief-of-staff of the defense force of the UAE. He will probably be replaced by an Abu Dhabian; in the meantime, the European link continues with Sheikh Zayed's sons being trained at Sandhurst in Britain.

Some Iranian scholars, in assessing the stability of the Shah's regime, discount a challenge from the left, but they do concede the possibility of a coup from the right, by the army. But this would be difficult to mount as the Shah takes a keen interest in his army and personally makes all appointments above a certain rank. Moreover, there are at least three intelligence organizations—his special office, the military intelligence network, and the State Security and Information Organization (SAVAK)—reporting to him personally. Others who report to the

Shah directly are the air-force commander, the chief-of-staff, the minister of war, the heads of the gendarmerie, city police, and imperial guard. In this manner, their reports can be checked and cross-checked. Politically ambitious officers in the Iranian armed forces, if they exist, will need to be extraordinarily devious in order to succeed. Iran offers some disturbing examples of the growth of security networks: those of the palace, the army, the police, and private channels. This proliferation of intelligence systems occurs in most of the Gulf states. If the country is united with a strong nationalistic current, the networks will pull together because everyone's first interest is the country. But more often, the agencies compete, clawing one another with such dedication that as organs of national security they are seriously weakened.

On the whole, tensions in the Gulf states between the armed forces and the civilian elite have remained at a low level; the exception is Iraq. In its early stages the Iraqi army became an instrument for nation-building, but it very soon became the preserve of the Sunni elite, which made it vulnerable to factionalism. The emergence of Baathist ideology aggravated the latent hostilities because the army, aware of its unpopularity, used the Baath party to enlist civilian support. But the party itself was divided, and when it was superimposed upon the army it led to "the emergence of divergent groups, and esoteric military cabals each contending for Baathist leadership" (Kelidar, 1975).

Between 1958-1966, the Iraqi leadership was dominated by the army. The situation began to change with the appointment of Saddam Hussein, who worked his way up to the position of vice-chairman of the Revolutionary Command Council (RCC) and heir apparent. Since then continuous purges of the military have in fact left the party in control of the armed forces. President al-Bakr, who was one of the leaders of the officers' revolt against Qasim in 1963, now enjoys the dual roles of secretary-general of the Baath party and field-marshal of the Iraqi armed forces. As a result he is in a position to promote either the civilian or the military faction when it suits him. But the degrading and savage purges that have permeated Iraq's politics since 1958 have created a rift and opened scores that are unlikely to terminate the infighting between suspicious military factions supported by distrustful and cynical politicians.

The intervention of the Iraqi army into politics, as in most countries, has led to the deterioration of the quality of political leadership—not that it was particularly distinguished in the first place. Those now in power are men of limited diplomatic vision and talent. An army that spends time politicizing loses its professional edge; the Iraqi armed forces revived some of that edge when they put down the Kurdish insurgency. If stability is maintained and the army is kept away from the centers of power, then its professional qualities could improve. But will it be content to be kept at a distance?

Subversion

In July 1975, Gulf foreign ministers met in Jeddah and endorsed, in principle, a defense summit. One of the six issues examined was mutual assistance against subversion and cooperation in military and intelligence affairs. In the recent past, pan-Arab radicalism, Baathism, and communism have had varying degrees of influence in the Gulf. But none of the regional leaderships has been forced to abdicate by such influence. In places, a ruler may be sufficiently popular, tolerant, or dextrous to avoid criticism; where oligarchies exist, their members are more interested in trade and development than politicizing (Center for Mediterranean Studies, 1972). Therefore, domestic subversion is less of a security problem than that generated from foreign sanctuaries. In this way local grievances are vulnerable to exploitation by external forces.

In the Gulf area there are only two communist parties, the Iraq Communist Party (ICP), and the Iranian Tudeh Party (Party of the Masses). The ICP's current membership is estimated at about 2,000, and since its foundation in 1943 it has had a turbulent passage. Between 1958 and 1972, the ICP and ruling

Baathists regarded each other with mutual suspicion. During this period some 3,000 communists were reported to have been killed, imprisoned, or expelled. The ICP's prospects improved slightly in 1972 when, under Soviet pressure, it accepted the offer of power-sharing made by the Baathists. Two communist members were appointed to the Cabinet and a year later the ICP was legalized for the first time in its history. But the ICP Cabinet members were little more than ineffectual civil servants. On important policy matters they were not consulted; in March 1975, the Iraqi leadership signed an accord with Iran that took the Soviet Union and the ICP completely by surprise. Baathists had been moving into the northern areas and had gained complete control of the Kurdish areas, at the expense of local communists. ICP offices were closed, and the opening of new offices was forbidden.

At times the alliance between Baathists and the ICP has given transient stability to the regime, but the relationship between the two parties has been "characterized by blood and vengeance" (Kelidar, 1975). The Baathists regard communism as a threat to Arab culture and the local communists as hired agents. The only point they can agree upon is united opposition against Western imperialism; but since March 1975, the RCC has modified its ideological rigor by seeking Western technical aid for Iraq's development programs.

Hounded by the Baathists and left out of the decision-making, the ICP also suffers from internal divisions. There is a pro-Moscow faction—the "Central Committee"—and a pro-Peking faction—the "Central Command." The split emerged in 1964, when the ultra-left accused the ICP of opportunism and expediency. In the 1960s the Maoist Central Command was active as a rural insurgency in the middle Euphrates region but it was quickly contained. Currently, Central Command guerrillas operate fitfully in the south and have allied tactically with dissident Kurds in seeking support.

The ICP is opposed by the majority of the population, which is conservative, Muslim, and anticommunist. When communism has thrived in Iraq it has generally done so by rallying all those communities that oppose Sunni Arab primacy. Shiis in Iraq have had few political organizations to represent their interests and young Shii radicals have always been attracted by ideology, especially that of opposition groups like the ICP. The official Communist Party is led by Sunnis and Kurds who are primarily intellectuals and professional people. This provides a sectarian ingredient to ideological conflict; in 1963, the Shiite leaders of the ICP were singled out and killed by Baathists. Not surprisingly, the split in the ICP is along a north-south axis that corresponds with the Shii-Sunni territorial divisions.

Because of its position as junior partner in the RCC, the ICP's ideological credentials are severely tested because it is not the proletariat that dictates but the Baathist elite. The question is how long is the ICP prepared to endure its subordinate role? If the Baathists and the ICP fall out over power-sharing, the Baathists are quite capable of decimating ranks of the ICP. The latter may resort to armed resistance, to expediency and compromise, or may defect from the cabinet and form a tactical alliance with the Maoist Central Command and Kurdish dissidents. If this were to happen the Baathists would have a fight on their hands; but the regime is aware of this danger and has warned the ICP against any reconciliation between the two communist factions. In the future—as in the past—the ICP's political influence will be rigidly determined by Baathist dynamics, Kurdish dissidence, and Iraqi-Soviet relations. Its prospects are not cheerful, particularly because of Moscow's attitude toward Arab communist parties: since World War II they have all been expendable instruments of Soviet policy in the region.

In 1941, a group of German-educated Marxist intellectuals formed the present Tudeh Party of Iran. Following an assassination attempt on the Shah in 1949, the party was banned. Party activity is confined almost entirely to organizations operating outside Iran, and Tudeh membership is about 1,000. There are, however, about 15,000-20,000 Iranians associated with other Marxist-Leninist groups engaged in a wide variety of opposition activities. They are represented by four major organizations:

(1) the Revolutionary Tudeh Party (*Hezb-e Tudeh-e Iran*), formed in 1965 by a Marxist faction that had been expelled from the Tudeh party;

(2) the Organization of Marxist-Leninists (*Sazman-e Marxist-Leninist*), formed in 1967 by two Maoist defectors from Tudeh's Central Committee;

(3) the Guerrilla Organization of the Devotees of the People *(Cheraki Feda-ye Khalq)*, which emerged in 1971. (Most of its members were formally in the Youth Organization of Tudeh; they left following the differences over guerrilla tactics; this group is well organized and has committed a number of violent incidents against the government; since 1971, about 100 members of this group have either been killed in action or executed.);

(4) the section of the National Front *(Jebheh-e Melli)* that supported the late Dr. Mosaddeq and that has become Marxist since 1972.

Although all these groups are in active opposition to the Shah, the Tudeh party remains the largest single party committed to revolution.

The party's main platform is a need to politicize the masses and turn them against the regime. Its propaganda organ, the clandestine "Radio Iran Courier," broadcasts from the German Democratic Republic (GDR) and one of its recent exhortations was that opposition elements in Iran should join the regime and the police organizations for tactical purposes. Once successfully infiltrated, they were urged to subvert and destroy the system from within.

In Maoist terms, opposition to the Shah has reached stage two—guerrilla warfare (the Maoist trinity is subversion, guerrilla activities, then, finally, open warfare at a conventional level). It has been a fairly regular feature of Iranian politics since 1971. In February of that year, a small band of guerrillas attacked a gendarmerie post at Siakhal in the northern province of Gilan. In military terms the attack was indecisive but it became mythified in the guerrillas' hagiography. After two years, the guerrillas claimed to have killed over 200 "enemy troops, police and SAVAK thugs," to have carried out 81 bomb attacks, and to have expropriated over 40 banks. In May 1975, two U.S. advisers were killed by terrorists; a statement released by the guerrillas claimed that the assassinations were in retaliation for nine prisoners shot in April. Although terrorist activity has continued, there were signs that by the summer of 1975, Iranian security forces had begun to close in on the terrorist networks. At the end of June 1975, police and guerrillas clashed in a town west of Tehran and four guerrillas and a policeman died. The following month, in the town of Meshed in the north, a terrorist sabotage group lost two men and two were captured in a shootout with police. Since mid-1975 there has been a marked diminution in terrorist activities, and in early 1976 the campaign against leftist activities continued. In January, 10 terrorists were shot for murdering the U.S. advisers and two Marxists were executed for planting bombs in a college.

One of the most articulate of the foreign-based dissenting voices is that coordinated by the Confederation of Iranian Students (C.I.S.) based in West Germany; one of its most active branches is the British section, the Iranian Student Society in Great Britain. Frequently, C.I.S. has attempted to disrupt the Shah's state visits to European countries and the United States. All the domestic and exiled opposition groups have a common anti-Shah program. Most of them have given up the idea of rural warfare with peasant support because the theorists argue that models of guerrilla warfare are irrelevant to Iranian society; one of the groups stated that "the indifference of the peasants is due to their lack of political awareness." Consequently Iranian dissidents advocate armed struggle in the form of "industrial strikes, sabotage of military and civilian institutions, and actions against the regime's institutions abroad."

In addition to urban terror tactics, Iranian terrorists have tried to aggravate ethnic and linguistic divisions within Iran. Within Iran's borders there are Kurds, Baluchis, Turks, and Arabs as well as Persians. One radical demand, after the creation of a People's Democratic Republic, was to foster equality among all the peoples of Iran. Guerrilla activity has occurred within Iranian Kurdistan. In March 1971, a gendarmerie helicopter was shot down; among those killed was Brigadier-General I. Sabet, chief of the gendarmerie in Kurdistan and Colonel Farbod, head of that force in Sanandaj, the major city in Kurdistan. In Sanandaj in January 1973, five guerrillas were arrested and charged with sabotage activity in Sanandaj and on roads in the area. The following year, guerrilla activity spread to the neighboring tribal province of Luristan.

But the guerrilla organizations are small; more serious in the long term is the escalation of student unrest in the universities into protracted and selective urban terrorism. The universities in Tehran—especially the Aryamehr Technical University—have experienced several serious riots; there have also been disturbances in Shiraz, Isfahan, and Tabriz. To all this, the government's reaction is draconian: secret trials, torture, summary executions. In the short term, a hard line may blunt the enthusiasm of urban guerrillas, but unless there is a serious attempt to redress the grievances, violence will be resumed but more strongly and with wider support.

Since the land reforms of the 1960s, the Shah has created several revolutionary corps to improve the quality of rural society. Young Iranians have a choice of serving in the rural corps instead of doing military service. After basic training, these young, professional, urban-bred recruits are sent to Iranian villages to implement their enthusiasms and skills. Many of the villages are sunk in poverty, ignorance, and illiteracy. There is mistrust on both sides, and inevitably the young idealists contrast the easier living of Tehran to the privations of the countryside. Some give up for selfish reasons; others are appalled and are motivated to bring equality and fairness. They begin to question the system that formed them and in time they perceive two Irans—the one of prestige projects and the other of inequality and deprivation. In a positive sense this indignation could be harnessed by the Iranian government and directed into channels for national development. But if the system chooses to ignore, or is unable to listen to the grievances, the guerrilla movement will have instant recruits. But it will not only be the left that will be talent-spotting; a reforming and ambitious army officer might see the opportunities presented by the existence of a frustrated intelligentsia and decide that his moment has come.

In the Gulf, Bahrain has generally been regarded as a political laboratory that was watched carefully by the other states. In June 1973, the government published an innovative constitution. It included several ideas that were revolutionary to the area. One of the most radical ideas was that the constitution, on acceptance, could not be changed by the electorate, their delegates, the ruler, or anyone else for the next five years. This was a clear restriction on the ruling family; also included were sections dealing with explosive socioeconomic issues such as equality for women, trade union rights, and the authority of the elected representatives to have control over the state's national resources. Most important of all, the creation of a National Assembly of 30 elected delegates and the Council of Ministers as ex-officio representatives, established Bahrain's supreme law-making authority. The 1973 election campaign for the Assembly was lively and sharply contested with 116 candidates competing. Several issues were ventilated: inflation, housing, national resources, and Gulf unity were promoted by Sunnis, Shias, Baathists, Arab nationalists, and Marxists. But the ruling al-Khalifah received a nasty shock because the results showed that the electorate was more radical than expected and almost half the total delegates chosen were either socialist or nationalist. An indication was the selection as speaker of the Assembly of Hasan Jawad al-Jishi. Al-Jishi, a Shia who had been arrested and exiled by the British 20 years ago, is a pronounced nationalist. The Assembly's first term was meant to run until 1977, but within two years it ran into problems. Trouble began in October 1974 over five or six bills dealing with housing, land, and labor laws. By May 1975, Assembly cooperation broke down completely; a logjam of legislation built up and in institutional terms there was no government. In August 1975, Sheikh Isa dissolved the National Assembly, and there seems little chance of it being recalled. It now seems clear that the radicalization of what had seemed like a good idea at the time had dispersed the ruler's enthusiasm for it. In the meantime, cost of living and housing grievances are escalating. There seems no doubt that a unique political experiment has ended. Some Bahrainis assert that the experiment was closely followed by Saudi Arabia, which was unhappy at the germination of political democracy in the Gulf. The same Bahrainis suspect that the Bahrain and Saudi establishments colluded in the idea of dissolving the Assembly.

Bahrain's nationalists and radicals are now discontented and frustrated politicians. Their dissidence may unite them and the future structure of political participation is unlikely to appease them. In the event the Assembly is irretrievably dissolved, the constitution may change; that is, some representatives will be elected and others will be nominated. The result will be an ineffective and purposeless debating chamber that will rubber-stamp all decisions made by the ruler. There will probably be a constitutional crisis in Bahrain in which those excluded from policy-making will put up a stiff resistance. It could even escalate into riots and violence, and if uncontrolled, unanticipated, or mismanaged could unseat the al-Khalifah dynasty.

In the states in the lower Gulf, some observers have been uneasy at the number of indigenous students who have been educated in the Soviet Union, East Europe, China, or the radical capitals of the Middle East such as Algiers, Baghdad, or Damascus. In 1974, Oman had 36 students at technical institutes in Warsaw Pact countries; on the whole they have not been a problem and have fitted in smoothly on their return to Oman. But some administrators in Muscat have lingering doubts that some of the ideology may have stuck. Perhaps the richest vein for subversive activity is located in the UAE. If it is assumed that inequality could lead to instability, then the embryonic federation may face serious problems in the next five years. Until recently, a rough estimate of the UAE's population was around 300,000, but a census in early 1976 revealed a much higher figure of 600,000. The detailed results were not published because the implications are serious. For instance, what was the proportion of native citizens of the UAE to immigrants? A "guesstimate" would be that immigrants and expatriates form nearly two-thirds of the UAE's population. With an overstretched administration, the UAE must hope to control immigration. Some selectivity has been introduced in job candidature; preference is given to a native Abu Dhabian, followed by a Gulf Arab, a northern Arab (that is, Syrian, Jordanian, Egyptian, or Sudanese), and finally a European or American. In the nature of things a self-aggrandizing elite forms around the ruling family. Many of the leading figures in this circle are political exiles from their own countries; others are there simply for the money although there are now discernible limits to amassing large personal fortunes. The national cakes are not getting any larger but more and more people want a slice. It will be the excesses of importuners that will assist the transient elite.

Because of the pressures and pace of development it is becoming more and more difficult to get through to the head of state. A good system of local government would do a great deal to meet the popular needs but there are now signs that in the states of the lower Gulf popular complaints are no longer getting through to the ruling elite. This faulty communication network is aggravated by the inclination of the time-servers at court to pass on only the good news or to make palatable (but falsify) the bad news. There are expatriate Arabs in key positions whose political survival depends on the tranquil disposition of their royal employers. Therefore, they have no interest in disturbing that condition. They are playing a dangerous game; some Arab advisers and technocrats assume a cultural superiority over their employers and the state they serve. They are easily bored for there is little intellectual excitement in the Gulf for political animals. Consequently, the traditional game of playing off factions becomes more serious as the rudimentary institutions of the developing states are impeded, manipulated, or corrupted by cynical expatriate Arabs. As nationalism develops in the smaller emirates, this type of adviser's capacity for mischief will increase. As state ministers begin to consult with each other over items such as Gulf currency, pollution, visa regulations, and so on, the traditional advisers are consulted less and less. At some point such an adviser may feel influence and power slipping away from him, so to recover his ground, he may conclude that it is time the independent ruler who employed him should be replaced by a more pliable man who would listen to advice. It is conceivable that as expatriates form an increasing majority in the UAE, they may reach a position of unassailable authority and intrigue for the succession of a regime that will perpetuate their interests at the expense of those of the indigenous citizen. In effect, the subversive activities of expatriate Arabs in the Gulf states could turn these states into little more than overseas clubs of Egyptians, Iraqis, Sudanese, or Somalis. This development could have significant regional consequences; the impact of internal pressures for political change in foreign relations in the Gulf is steadily increasing. If change were to occur as a result of sectional and ethnic interests, the foreign policy of a northern Arab lobby would be entirely different from that of a national from Qatar, UAE, or Oman.

For the moment, although radical political ideas have had some influence in the Gulf, they have been overtaken by the development programs of regional states that have created more throughgoing social and economic revolutions than any imported ideology. But there is no guarantee that this will always be the case. These programs are inevitably narrowly-based and they are alarmingly vulnerable to mismanagement, overenthusiasm, or inertia. Controlled change in the Gulf is probably the best guarantee against subversion, but none of the states have the time. They are all in a hurry.

IV. EXTERNAL PROBLEMS

Arab-Iranian Relations

U ntil 1968, Iranian policy toward the Arab states of the Gulf was passive and unimaginative. Although the Shah antici-pated that Britain would eventually withdraw from the Gulf, the timing of the British announcement (January 16, 1968) left Iran totally unprepared diplomatically. Its military programs were well advanced but Iran had no diplomatic machinery—area specialists and linguists—and no Gulf or Bahrain policy. The British an-nouncement came at a time when Arab leaders were already exchanging visits; on January 17, the ruler of Bahrain concluded a three-day visit to Saudi Arabia and secured a pledge of complete support "in all circumstances" (Chubin and Zabih, 1974). This pledge, subsequent visits between Arab leaders, and the British decision to create a federation of smaller emirates aroused the Shah's suspicion of an Arabian Gulf. He revived a territorial claim to Bahrain and declared his opposition to the island's inclusion in any federation. A dangerous Arab-Iranian dispute was averted when the United Nations negotiated independent statehood for Bahrain in 1970, which satisfied all parties. In November 1971, the Shah's concern—to maintain freedom of navigation in the Straits of Hormuz—led to the occupation of a group of islands at the mouth of the Gulf, Abu Musa (owned by Sharjah) and the Tumbs (owned by Ras al-Khaimah). The seizure of the islands provoked anti-Iranian riots in some of the lower Gulf states; Iraq severed diplomatic relations with Iran and Britain over the incident. For a short time, Saudi Arabia, Kuwait, and Iraq threatened military action against Iran. Further afield, Libya, suspecting British-Iranian collusion, used the incident as a pretext for nationalizing British Petroleum's (BP) Libyan concessions.

Iran's military strength dominates the Gulf, and this only aggravates the semantic arguments over the Arabian or Persian Gulf. The Shah has a Gaullist-like conception of Iran's place in history in which Persia's past greatness and historical heritage are significant. Since the nineteenth century, Persian ambition has been obstructed by preoccupation with Russia, British presence, and lack of a navy. In the late 1970s the position has altered to such an extent that the Shah has become eminently quotable on the subject: "Iran's supremacy over the Persian Gulf is a natural thing. We already have this and we shall enhance it in the future" (Chubin and Zabih, 1974).

Arab attitudes toward Iran are mixed: many Arab leaders are privately derogatory about the Shah's military policies; some are anxious at Iran's strategic ambitions—the view of Iraq, Saudi Arabia, and possibly Kuwait and Qatar; while others, such as Oman, express a feeling of security because they enjoy Iranian military assistance and protection. The Arab reservations toward Iran's military strength are mildly disingenuous because there have been Iranian advisers in the Arabian peninsula since 1962. During the Yemen civil war (1962-1969), the Shah sent supplies, advisers, and observers to the Royalist side. As all the war material was channelled via Saudi Arabia it could only have been done with Saudi approval.

Yet Arab suspicions are not allayed. Twice in the last two years, the Shah has called on the Arab states to join him in some kind of regional defense pact. On both occasions there was a stunning silence. The paradox in the Arab position is best illustrated by the case of Oman. Regional Arab cooperation, in the form of aid and mediation, has done a great deal to assist Oman in defeating PFLO; but it can be argued that Iranian military support has done more. Since 1973, numerous press reports have mentioned particularly Saudi opposition to Iranian troops in Oman, but in that time no formal Saudi complaint has been made either to Muscat or Tehran. Nevertheless a discreet diplomatic push for influence is apparent in Iranian and Saudi policies. In March 1976, King Khalid paid an extensive visit to several Gulf states. This marked a new activism in Saudi policy and included the first visit to Abu Dhabi by a Saudi ruler—a highly significant inter-Arab event. A few weeks earlier the Shah had recalled his ambassadors in the Gulf states following a decision by the latter to create an Arabian Gulf news agency.

Since March 1975, Iran's Arab policy has been encouraged by the accord with Iraq. That accord did a great deal to lower tensions in the area, although regional attitudes toward it vary from euphoria to skepticism. The skeptics are important as they include some of Iraq's Baathist extremists. These dissenters protest that Iraq conceded too much to Iran and that the Iraqi Baath has handed over the Gulf to permanent Iranian hegemony. The Baathists are now aware that they were outmaneuvered by the Shah, whose diplomacy and financial aid to Arab countries won him allies and support. It also prevented Iraq from Arabizing its dispute with Iran. The dissatisfied Baathists in Baghdad, given the opportunity, could upset Arab-Iranian rapprochement in the Gulf.

Dormant grievances between Iran and the Gulf states include ethnic, sectarian, dynastic, linguistic, and territorial problems. Basically, all the grievances are the result of the clash between Arabian and Iranian nationalism. Some Arab nationalists have tried to influence anti-Iranian attitudes by claiming that the Iranian occupation of the islands and the presence of Iranians in the lower Gulf are simply a prelude to an eventual Iranian invasion and occupation of the Arab Gulf. On the whole, the Iranian immigrants are generally not political, and their most influential representatives, the merchants, are usually allied with the Arab establishment. At a higher level, members of the ruling families frequently visit southern Iran on hunting trips or for holidays. An important factor in the stabilization of Arab-Iranian relations is the quality of Iranian diplomatic representation. Without exception the Iranian ambassadors to the Gulf states are cosmopolitan, considerate, and polished. The Iranians are conscious of their military superiority and take pains to be conciliatory.

Currently the most sensitive issue between Iran and the Gulf states is the sharp difference over oil prices. Iran has pressed for higher prices to fund its huge development program for its large population, but Saudi Arabia has chosen to peg or even lower prices. In February, Iran was obliged to meet the majority demands and cut its price of heavy crude oil by 9.5 U.S. cents a barrel. Other Gulf producers such as Iraq and Kuwait had previously lowered their prices of heavy crude oil in order to improve their sales. There were other global factors at work in the oil market, but the pan-Arab lobby used the occasion as a vindication of Arab policies against Iranians in OPEC. Nevertheless, Arab resistance to higher prices and a depressed energy consumption market compelled the Shah, in August 1976, to negotiate oil-for-arms barter arrangements with Britain and the United States.

Given the historical nature of many of the problems between Iran and the Arab states, one of the most encouraging developments is that the evolution of Iranian regional policy is becoming increasingly acceptable to the Arabs. Until 1974-1975, Iranian policy toward the Gulf states was predominantly military. But since then there has emerged a regional trend of subordinating security issues in favor of social, economic, and political development. At the moment, Iran's Gulf policy is to encourage economic cooperation among the regional states and to foster self-reliance.

Territorial Claims

Since 1971, territorial disputes have lost their edge: Iran has relinquished its claim to Bahrain, and in 1974 Saudi Arabia and Abu Dhabi reached agreement over the Buraimi Oasis and other parts of Abu Dhabi's territory. Sharjah appears to have accepted the loss of Abu Musa to Iran for the time being, but there are still people in Ras al-Khaimah who resent the occupation of their islands.

Of the remaining disputes, that between Kuwait and Iraq is the most combustible. In 1961, General Qasim claimed Kuwait, a challenge that was defeated by British troops and Arab League forces. Eventually Kuwait had to pay U.S. $70 million to buy off Iraq's claim, though the demarcation of frontiers has yet to be completed. In 1973, there were clashes between Iraqi and Kuwaiti forces when the Iraqis seized the Kuwaiti border post of al-Samita. Kuwait called on Saudi troops to assist its own forces to protect the border. The dispute is unresolved and Kuwait is vulnerable to Iraqi pressure tactics. There has been some progress in the dispute because Iraq has offered to supply Kuwait with fresh water in return for leasing arrangements for the islands of Bubiyan and Warbah. Kuwait's suspicion of Iraq is one reason why Kuwait would prefer to settle its border with Iraq before joining any collective security arrangement. "Kuwait supports any measure that increases the security of the Gulf and any method of achieving this aim *provided* all existing problems between the states have been settled (Middle East International, 1976). While Iraq is pursuing a more moderate policy in the region the dispute will remain dormant; but if the regime in Baghdad feels strong enough, or needs a face-saving foreign adventure, another border incident cannot be ruled out.

Arguably, Kurdish dissidence is a domestic problem for Iraq, but during the 11-month war (April 1974-March 1975) the involvement of external powers—the Soviet Union, Iran, and the United States—threatened to internationalize the insurgency. On

March 6, 1975, Iraq and Iran signed an agreement in Algiers that settled a number of long-standing border questions, defined navigation rights in the Shatt-el-Arab, and brought to an end Iranian support for the Kurdish rebellion. While some Kurdish units fought on in small-scale guerrilla groups, about 20,000 Kurds responded to an amnesty offered by Iraq and about 40,000 fled into Iran; among the latter was the Kurdish leader Mullah Mustafa Barzani. The Algiers agreement was followed by a state visit of the Iranian foreign minister to Iraq on June 15, and by the signing of a "reconciliation" treaty that settled all outstanding grievances between the two countries.

The Iraqi government's policy toward the Kurds after the accord was vigorous but not vengeful. Some Kurdish leaders were alleged to have disappeared in mysterious circumstances, but what evidence has emerged indicated that old scores were being settled between Arabs and Kurds. Baghdad pushed through tough land reforms in Kurdish areas and began to centralize all administration in the region, which had been loosely autonomous—a policy that was designed to forcibly assimilate the Kurds with the Iraqi system. Other measures included the large-scale transfer of Kurds to southern Iraq in the lower Tigris towns of Amara and Nasryia. But some Kurdish groups refused to accept defeat, and in June and July 1976, there were unconfirmed reports of renewed fighting between hit-and-run Kurdish guerrillas and Iraqi forces. By 1976, the Kurdish attacks were only of nuisance value. If the attacks increase in number and strength, the Kurds are unlikely to receive Iranian support, nor would they trust the Shah even if support were offered. Therefore, the Kurds would be at the mercy of the Iraqi forces. The accord of 1975 undoubtedly saved the Kurds from being decimated, because all the signs indicated that the Baghdad regime was preparing to destroy the Kurdish problem once and for all. In territorial terms, there seems virtually no hope of the Kurds recovering lost ground; as a lightweight guerrilla force the Kurds could fight on indefinitely but with diminishing returns.

Gulf Radicals

Pan-Arab radicalism has lost much of its horsepower since the 1950s and 1960s, and for the time being the disruptive influence of Baghdad's Baathists and Aden's Marxists has diminished. One of the results of the Iraq-Iran accord was that Iraq ended its anti-Iranian invective and cross-border raids. Since 1975, Baghdad has embarked on a massive diplomatic offensive in the region— and in the Arab world generally—to improve its image by organizing trade fairs, joint venture deals, and increased diplomatic representation. All the regional states welcome the new image, but equally, they are all vigilant. They all remember that between 1958 and 1975 Iraq caused problems in the Arab-Israeli dispute, in Oman, Kuwait, Iran, and Pakistan.

The architect of Iraq's current constructive attitude is Saddam Hussein. As long as his position is secure, his policy will continue. What must be considered is whether Iraq's moderation will survive his departure. The country's infrastructure is rudimentary, and it needs all the money and assistance it can get for development. In 1975 Iraq was the only regional oil producer that did not reduce its output. For the moment, Iraq seems to be devoting its resources to development and not revolution. One Arab statesman said of Iraq that "while they're making money they won't throw bombs." The signs are cautiously encouraging: in February 1976, Iraq took the initiative in renewing diplomatic links with Oman. In the past, Baghdad had been a principal supporter of PFLO; like other states, Oman welcomed the initiative but will keep up its guard. There are Iraqis who work in the Gulf who could, conceivably, become Baathist agents, but most of them have cast their lot with the traditional systems. These include an unknown number of Gulf Arabs who were educated in Iraqi institutions. Another positive sign is that the Iraqi media no longer carry PFLO statements.

Since the Iraq-Iran accord, Baghdad has devoted most of its resources to internal development. Like Algeria, Iraq is probably the only oil-producing country that needs every cent of its oil revenues for national projects; in some cases—as in June 1975—Iraq borrowed nearly U.S. $700 million from Europe and Saudi Arabia for its industrial program. In that same month an agreement was signed with the Soviet Union for the execution of 15 industrial, agricultural, and irrigation projects in Iraq. In its drive for modernity, the ruling RCC is convinced that complete socialization of the economic system is desirable, but it is questionable whether it is efficient. In its zeal, the government approved in March 1976 a draconian law concerning agencies and the private sector that frightened off many private Western companies, whose skills and technical assistance are desperately needed. By autumn 1976, the RCC was clearly having second thoughts about the proper climate for foreign investment, and an unreported debate has already begun within the RCC between those who want more socialization and development and those who would prefer to use the oil revenues for fueling subversion. If this debate is protracted it could lead to a paralysis in the economic programs leading in turn to a power struggle.

In these circumstances the last thing the RCC wants is a Kurdish revival; in early 1976, a series of serious incidents were reported in northern Iraq between Kurdish civilians and Iraqi militia who tried to resettle the Kurds in less sensitive areas of Iraq. By March, a new Kurdish splinter moverment had emerged— the National Union of Kurdistan (NUK), led by Jalal Talabani— which is opposed to the Kurdistan Democratic Party formerly led by Mustafa Barzani. Significantly, the NUK formed in Damascus, a united-front movement with six exiled Iraqi Arab parties, mainly communists. The appearance of the NUK accelerated Baghdad's zeal in resettling the Kurds and clearing them from border areas. Pro-regime Kurds live in an uneasy alliance with the Baathists and there has been negligible progress in implementing Kurdish autonomy. Shortly after the accord, a number of Kurds who had returned from Iranian sanctuary were executed by Iraq, which claimed they were "double agents." By May-June, the tense relationship between the RCC and the Kurds had snapped as serious clashes occurred between Iraqi forces and Kurdish guerrillas. Kurdish spokesmen in London told the author in June that the NUK/KDP had been reorganized along socialist/Marxist principles and was planning a sustained guerrilla campaign in the mountains. The NUK/KDP claimed that the Kurds had been compelled to take up arms as a result of the forcible deportation of 300,000 of their number from Kurdish areas to southern Iraq. The fighting has been on a small scale and is likely to remain so; the largest skirmishes took place in the Mosul and Dohuk areas of northern Iraq. Some unconfirmed reports alleged that some armed Kurds had trickled back across the border from Iran. The presence of Kurdish irredentists in Iran and the threat of renewed, more intensive clashes, led to secret talks in August between Iraq and Iran. These were followed by a new amnesty to Kurdish refugees in Iran to return to safety to Iraq. At the same time Iran exerted considerable pressure on its Kurdish exiles to accept the offer. Moreover, Iran agreed to close down the last remaining Kurdish refugee camp near Shiraz.

Externally, Iraqi-Syrian relations, never friendly because of ideological and economic differences, became openly hostile as a result of the Lebanese civil war. Since as early as 1962, even the Russians have been trying to mediate between both countries in the dispute over the Euphrates, the waters of which are now controlled by Syria's Soviet-built dam at Tabqa. Nor have the Russians been successful in resolving the dispute between the two countries over the flow of oil through the Syrian pipeline to the Mediterranean. In northern Iraq, the oil now bypasses Syria in a new pipeline through Turkey (Kirkuk-Dortyol). Syria's attempts to prevent the partition of Lebanon were treated with suspicion in Baghdad, and when Syrian troops entered Lebanon in June those suspicions seemed to be confirmed. Iraq expressed its concern at the Syrian attempt, via the Syrian-sponsored Palestinian movement *Saiqa*, to bring the PLO* under Syrian control. Predictably, the Iraqis via the ALF** supported the "rejection front" and all those parties opposed to Syrian intervention.

The deteriorating relationships between Baghdad and Damascus created a bizarre incident in the Gulf. In April, Saddam

*Palestine Liberation Organization
**Arab Liberation Front

Hussein was due to pay a visit to Saudi Arabia, Kuwait, Bahrain, Qatar, and UAE. On April 12, the RCC met after receiving information that a Syrian plan to assassinate Hussein in a Gulf state had been discovered. This meant that the Gulf tour was altered and Saddam Hussein only visited Saudi Arabia. This in itself was important because the visit to Riyadh was the first by such a senior Iraqi minister since 1958. Saddam Hussein had talks with King Khalid and Crown Prince Fahd, and they dealt exclusively with Lebanon, especially Syrian involvement. It seems probable that the Iraqi visit to Saudi Arabia was an attempt to Arabize the Lebanese dispute and minimize the Syrian role.

But any cordiality that may have attended the Iraqi-Saudi meeting was rapidly dispelled. By July, Iraqi officials were attacking Saudi Arabia in strong terms following disagreements over oil pricing. At an OPEC conference in June, Saudi Arabia refused to support an overall increase in prices for crude petroleum. The Iraqi ministers of petroleum, planning, and information, launched bitter and concerted attacks on the Saudi position. In an interview with the *Washington Post* (July 26), Minister for Information Tariq Aziz stated: "we wanted to build good close relations with Saudi Arabia but, unfortunately, the Saudi government is following an oil policy which Iraq cannot accept." Bothered by Kurds, problems of financing development programs, hostile Syrians, and cagey Gulf states, Iraq once again may feel surrounded by enemies. There is a body of opinion maintaining that, in such circumstances, Iraq may resume its role as the subversive center of the Gulf, but Western businessmen think that Iraq is too deeply committed to national development to find time for political mischief-making.

Since 1967, the PDRY has been the only serious Marxist regime in the area. In its support for the PFLO insurgency in Oman's Dhofar province, Aden has provided every kind of assistance, from indoctrination to military training. Before it was defeated, PFLO's seven-man central committee was based in Aden. Recruitment into PFLO was done at an early age; by a combination of coercion and invitation, *jabali* children were sent to the People's School—formerly Lenin School—at al-Gheidha. The school had a capacity of 700-800, and the pupils were taught English, science, geography, engineering, and political indoctrination. Further training in weaponry and fieldcraft was provided at the Revolutionary Training Camp near Hauf. Hard-core PFLO recruits then went to the Soviet Union for further training. Financing for the movement was mainly provided by the PDRY in the form of a monthly budget or through donations from PFLO members and supporters. The PDRY also provided the PFLO with passports, and its Kuwait embassy was used to maintain contact with PFLO members in the Gulf. East Germany assists in training the PDRY police and security forces, and Cuba mainly trains pilots and gives some military and medical instruction (Price, 1975). In January 1976, the Oman government reported that about 280 PDRY regular troops were operating in west Dhofar. But a month earlier—in December 1975—the PFLO had been militarily defeated, and by late 1976 Oman could claim total military security in Dhofar.

For years the Aden-based "Voice of Oman" had broadcast PFLO propaganda, but by 1974 it was apparent to even the most doctrinaire ideologist that PFLO was losing the war. By the summer of that year, following a gloomy fourth congress of the PFLO, the PDRY's economic condition was critical; there were increasing signs that the PDRY was more interested in putting its own house in order rather than fomenting revolution in neighboring territories. President Sadat's moderation, plus a loan from Abu Dhabi during this period, may have convinced the PDRY that its political and economic survival was better served by allying with conservative Arab states than by supporting importunate and costly guerrillas.

Aden's last throw began in August 1974; then, after the fourth congress, the PFLO decided to revert to phase one of Mao's tactics—a campaign of subversion and propaganda in the centers of population. After that meeting and the announcement of a change in strategy, some kind of operation was expected by the Omani authorities. One indication was the absence of Abdulla

Humaid al Ghassan, a member of PFLO's central committee, from Aden for the month of August. He is believed to have been in northern Oman. At that time of year the heat is enervating, tempers are short, petty grievances escalate, and to a casual observer, the country might appear ripe for revolution. On October 29, 1974, a Land Rover was stopped at a military checkpoint on a road near Rostaq; in an exchange of fire two people were wounded: a soldier and one of the passengers, Zahir Ali Matar al-Miyahi (alias Ahmed Ali), a member of PFLO's central committee. The vehicle contained four others, including another central committee member. They were carrying a large sum of money, weapons, and explosives; there was evidence that the unit was planning an assassination. The Rostaq group had been trained by the Popular Front of the Liberation of Palestine (PFLP) in a refugee camp near Beirut.

As the war came to an end, regional Arab diplomacy began to make some impression on the PDRY's intransigence. In 1974, the island of Perim, owned by Aden, was placed at Egypt's disposal. The deal will cost US $10 million annually, which will be paid by Saudi Arabia. The Arabs made several gains from this deal:

(1) the control of Perim could be used for an anti-Israel blockade in the event of renewed hostilities;

(2) it is a convenient cover for aid to the PDRY in an attempt to offset Soviet influence in the PDRY and the Somali Democratic Republic; and

(3) the buying of a piece of PDRY real estate may help to prime the pump for wider international aid to the state.

This policy seems to have been successful: in March 1976, Saudi Arabia and PDRY announced an intention to resume diplomatic relations. It is expected that Arab money will now begin to reach Aden. Currently the PDRY's interest in PFLO seems to have fallen sharply for a number of reasons:

(1) Aden sees no future in supporting a defeated movement;

(2)   the PDRY is having second thoughts about its position in the Arab world;

(3)   the Soviet Union may have lost interest and switched its attention to the Horn of Africa and Southern Africa; and

(4)   PDRY and PFLO may have run out of ammunition and other military supplies.

The "hiccups" in Aden's support for the insurgency also had domestic causes. Since 1967, the ruling elite in the PDRY has rarely enjoyed anything like harmonious unity. In October 1975, the United National Front Political organization (UNFP) was formed as a result of a merger between the ruling Marxist National Front, the pro-Soviet Democratic People's Union Party (DPUP), comprising former members of the government; and the Popular Vanguard Party (PVP), formed by disaffected Baathists. The merger came after five years of acrimonious debate and reflected the PDRY's closer alignment with the Soviet Union. In conciliating the various Marxist factions, a major role was played by Naif Hawatmah, leader of the PDFLP. The secretary-general of the UNFP is Abdul Fattah Ismail and the chairman is Salim Rubai Ali, both of whom are protagonists in a power struggle between the Maoists (Rubai Ali) and the pro-Moscow faction (Fattah Ismail). Significantly, the unification congress avoided any criticisms of Saudi Arabia, nor did it mention the power shifts in the Yemen Arab Republic (YAR). In fact, when asked to comment about events in Sana, Abdul Fattah Ismail said that the PDRY's relations with the YAR were better than at any time in the past and that they were constantly improving.

It now seems clear that Egyptian and Iraqi pressure was responsible for moderating Aden's policy. In the spring of 1975, Iraq promised Aden a large loan as a contribution toward the PDRY's five-year plan on condition that Aden end its support for PFLO. In addition, Iraq tried to clear the air between the PDRY and Saudi Arabia. Iraq's motives were fairly obvious and displayed a great deal of common sense. Following the Iraq-Iran accord, Iraq decided that in the Gulf its continued support for Aden would:

(1) tarnish its new-found image as peacemakers;

(2) provoke the hostility of Saudi Arabia; and

(3) draw Iran deeper into the internal affairs of the Arab states of the lower Gulf.

PDRY's position became awkward and remains so; at the end of 1974, its trade deficit was US $106 million despite the cancellation in August 1974 of a Soviet debt of U.S. $50 million.

In pan-Arab terms, the PDRY's ideological fervor has abated slightly but opponents of the regime receive short shrift. British sources estimate that there are about 10,000 political prisoners in the PDRY; the numbers executed or unaccounted for are inestimable and the East German-trained security network is effective, and for the moment, immovable. In October 1975, Muhammad Ali Haitham—a former prime minister in the PDRY—survived an assassination attempt in Cairo. The unsuccessful gunmen were arrested by the Egyptians and were found to be members of the PDRY security forces. In the area, Haitham's opposition to Rubai Ali was well-known, and such a tactless operation threatened to undo tentative South Arabian diplomatic initiatives.

Following the talks in March 1976 between Saudi Arabia and the PDRY, the ideological rivalry in Aden intensified. The Soviet Union increased its flag-waving naval visits to Aden. At the beginning of April there were three ships in port; the previous month there had been clashes between supporters of Salim Rubai Ali and those of Abdul Fattah Ismail at a UNFP branch meeting in Aden. Fighting broke out, shots were fired and several people were injured. In August, a military commander, Brigadier Mohammed Abdulla Marzaeah, survived assassination by poison and he was simply the latest victim of the UNFP's lethal disagreements.

It could well be that the fate of the PDRY will be determined by the paymaster. In the past, the Soviet Union has provided about U.S. $10 million in loans over five years and is the source of one-quarter of Aden's foreign aid. But this is a derisory sum when compared to the potential aid available from Saudi Arabia, and the Soviet Union cannot really compete in that respect.

Moreover, cash alone does not really meet the needs of the PDRY. It needs people who build things and in this regard the Chinese are infinitely more effective than the Russians; Chinese laborers are busy constructing a 300-mile road from Aden to Mukalla in appalling terrain, and in 1976 they are reported to be ahead of schedule. There is always the possibility that Aden will take the money and run but this is unlikely until the present power struggle is resolved.

Arab-Israeli Dispute

In the past, political events in the Gulf have occurred in spite of, not because of, the consequences of the Arab-Israeli dispute. As nation-states most of the Gulf countries have no direct interest in the dispute. There is no national territory involved nor are any of the states subject to Israeli attacks.

States such as Kuwait and the UAE with sizable Palestinian communities have built-in commitments; every Palestinian at work in the Gulf contributes about five percent of his annual earnings to the PLO. All Arab countries subsidize the PLO but in a way that is double-edged. Individual movements may claim that they have adequate funds but, since 1970, PLO treasurers have complained annually that Arab aid never really matches the promises. At one particularly acrimonious session in Cairo in January 1973, the PLO protested that Arab countries were nearly U.S. $40 million in arrears in payments to the PLO. Some Arab states have deliberately fostered one movement at the expense of another, forcing such a client to be subordinate to the national interest of its patron. Since October 1973, Iraq—supported by Libya—has sponsored a hawkish faction of the PLO, namely the PFLP, the PFLP General Command, and the Baathists' own organization, the Arab Liberation Front (ALF). The PLO is currently fighting for survival in Lebanon, but before the civil war the three groups had withdrawn from the PLO Executive Committee and formed the "rejection front." Iraq has financed and supported this front in order to mobilize Arab radical opinion against a compromise solution for the Middle East dispute. Iraq's main vehicle has been the ALF, which the Iraqi Baathists hope will form a rival PLO opposed to the al-Fatah—Saiqa-dominated body led by Yasir Arafat. But this seems unlikely because the ALF is all too clearly an expendable creation of the Iraqi state and the Baathists and is also seen as a rival to the Syrian-sponsored Saiqa.

The presence of thousands of Palestinians in the Gulf has alarmed some observers who fear that their commitment to Palestine will unsettle the traditional systems in the Gulf. But like the majority of expatriates, they are there for the money so they have an interest in maintaining and supporting the regime that pays them. Moreover, one has to distinguish which Palestinians one has in mind when talking of the adventitious effects of the Arab-Israeli dispute. Some are recognizably the "fat cats" of the revolution; others are industrious and extremely talented and play important roles in nation-building; and others are in refugee camps in Lebanon that are the real forcing-houses of revolution. Few Arab Gulf rulers express anxiety about Palestinian fifth columnists in their own infrastructures because those Palestinians are settled, and the indigenous security services are generally effective enough to detect incipient subversion—from any source.

Since 1973, the use of the oil weapon has locked Gulf producers into a new economic and political arrangement. The weight of Saudi Arabia determines the attitudes of the Arab states in the Gulf toward the Middle East dispute. Moreover, the principal Arab protagonist, Egypt, is heavily dependent on Saudi aid. Until further notice is given, Saudi Arabia has committed itself to Egypt, and if King Khalid applies sanctions, other Gulf states would support his action. Arab oil-producing countries have expressed solidarity with each other and they have all been convinced by the past success of the oil weapon. Furthermore, Arab oil producers have committed themselves to a solution of the Middle East dispute. Should another war be fought or negotiations continue to be stalemated—despite the decimation by the

Lebanese Christians of the Palestinians (in any settlement the status of Palestinians will still need to be negotiated)—then a new application of the oil weapon seems inevitable and the Gulf states, including Iran, will support the Saudi position (Maull, 1975).

The skill and sophistication with which the oil weapon was used signifies that in the future such a tactic will not be lightly employed. What has happened is that negotiations for a Middle East settlement must now include the probability of oil sanctions as part of a new oil diplomacy. A simple threat of sanctions is already apparent in the UN; the IMF; the World Bank; in the creation of the consumers club, the International Energy Agency (IEA); and in the demands of some U.S. analysts to retaliate by using agricultural exports as an instrument of economic warfare. The industrialized countries' dependence on oil will increase:

> The proved reserves of the world are not sufficient to satisfy growing market demands for very long. More than half will be needed in the next decade alone (1975-1985). The petroleum industry, therefore, must constantly replenish reserves as they are depleted by production. And it must find more each year than it produces [Chase Manhattan Bank, 1975].

Most Gulf oil producers are aware of their economic dependence and military weakness, but they also understand the considerable economic leverage they possess. Fortunately, the interdependence of consumers and producers is so obvious that few people are prepared to upset the equilibrium. But the urgency of seeking a solution to the Arab-Israeli dispute remains; in October 1973 an oil embargo achieved much more than force of arms. The implications are obvious to the principal peacemaker, the United States.

An interesting regional development, in the event of another war-inspired oil embargo, will be Iran's position. Iran has numerous links with Israel such as oil sales, intelligence and agricultural cooperation, a common arms supplier (the United States), and a distrust of Arab motives. The Shah has worked hard to improve his relations with Egypt, Saudi Arabia, and Syria but in a future war it seems unlikely that the Shah will have bought himself an independent position. In such a war, he would have to consider whether his interests in a largely Arab region are served by supporting Israel.

Soviet Policy in the Gulf

For the moment Soviet policy in the Gulf is in disarray. In 1972, Iraq and the Soviet Union signed a Treaty of Friendship that was a comprehensive arrangement. Four articles dealt specifically with mutual security arrangements, and until 1975 the Soviet Union was the principal supplier of technical and military assistance to Baghdad. But the treaty does not seem to have committed Iraq in any way. Iraq's communists are members of the ruling coalition but neither they nor Moscow have been able to penetrate the Takriti circle. The Iraq-Iran accord surprised the Soviet Union, and when Iraq began to turn to the West for technical assistance, Moscow temporarily suspended arms supplies in the early summer of 1975. Even when relations between Baghdad and Moscow were cordial, the Soviet Union had very little room for maneuver; it was careful not to place too much reliance on a highly unstable Iraqi coalition. In addition, Moscow's concern to maintain cordial relations with Iran dissuaded it from giving wholehearted support to Iraq's adventures. When Iraq's Kurdish insurgency was renewed in 1974, the Soviet Union enjoyed a fleeting importance as supplier and advisor to the Iraqi armed forces. Soviet reluctance to take sides in Arab-Iranian polemics does not mean that it will withdraw from the Gulf or that it will reduce its investment, slacken its drive for influence, or its efforts to weaken the West's influence. What the Soviet Union has been forced to relearn is that national leaderships are able to act unilaterally no matter how much aid they may have received from external powers.

At one stage Soviet involvement in the Gulf took the form of direct assistance to the PFLO. Its principal weapons were the AKM and AK47 (Kalashnikov) automatic and semiautomatic rifles, mortars, and antitank and antipersonnel mines. In 1974, in Salalah, the author interviewed a 19-year-old guerrilla with four years' training who had defected to the government side. He revealed how he, with 14 others, had spent several weeks at a training school in Odessa for instruction in weaponry, mainly the RCL rocket launcher and the SAM-7 missile. In February 1976, SAF units found a complete SAM-7B unfired and cached; launchers had been captured earlier, but not the missiles. It is possible that parity in the Gulf is not a Soviet aspiration; it is of secondary importance but is an extension of Soviet policy in the Indian Ocean. The Gulf itself had not been of direct strategic concern to the superpowers since the 1950s. At the moment, if the Gulf were isolated for bargaining purposes, the Soviet Union could not exert the leverage in the near future to weaken the Western position (Hurewitz, 1974). If the cold war were to escalate in the Gulf it would begin in the Indian Ocean.

Nevertheless, the Soviet Union will not lightly surrender the toeholds it has in the Gulf. In June 1976, Prime Minister Kosygin visited Iraq following improved economic relations between the two countries. In 1975, Soviet supplies of oil-prospecting equipment and military aircraft to Iraq (and Syria) improved, and in the first six months of 1976 there was a continuing upward trend. Despite Western successes in exports to Iraq, the Soviet Union is not prepared to be shunted aside. Soviet participation in Iraq's irrigation projects will continue for some time to come. Yet compared to 1975, Soviet investment in the area has diminished considerably; what is more, the traditional financial relationship in the area has altered. In March 1976, a Soviet mission visited Kuwait, led by the vice-president of the Central Bank. Both sides are reported to have discussed a U.S. $34 million loan to the Soviet Union along with joint ventures in the Third World. In the past, Kuwait has openly invited Soviet participation in the Kuwaiti oil industry. In December 1975, a cultural and scientific cooperation agreement was signed during the visit to Moscow of the Kuwait foreign minister, Sheikh Sabah al-Ahmad. It is an open secret that Kuwait has expressed interest in buying Soviet arms.

In the PDRY, Adenis have described the Soviet link as the PDRY's hair shirt; the Russians have been largely responsible for placing that country in a disastrous barter economy. And although PFLO's Soviet-supported campaign has failed, Moscow is unlikely to be dislodged from Aden without some resistance. Between March and June 1976, 10 Soviet delegations plus support teams visited Aden. As a result of the restoration of relations between PDRY and Saudi Arabia in March 1976, there is now a possibility that Aden will choose Saudi money in preference to Soviet ties. The joint communique between the two countries was quite euphoric, proclaiming "Arab brotherhood, good neighborliness, and non-intervention in each other's internal affairs." That remains to be seen; there are skeptics who believe that Aden will simply take the money, but continue with its doctrinaire policies. The choice will not be easy, because the PDRY has relied almost exclusively on Soviet economic aid. Technoexport is currently exploring for oil in the eastern area and there are already rumors of an oil strike. If it were realized, the losing game being played by the Soviet Union in the Gulf may well see another loss, this time in a rupture between Aden and Moscow.

Few Arab ministers in the Gulf believe that any of their Arab neighbors will become permanent clients of Moscow; but being Arabs, one or two ministers have sideswiped Iran. There was a great deal of anxiety in 1972 when Iraq signed the Friendship Treaty, but no one remarked on Iranian permission a year earlier for the Soviet Union to use a railway to Gulf ports. This really worried some Gulf leaders. Although the Shah may worry about the Soviet Union, it is probably more true to say that Moscow is deeply concerned at its inability to effectively influence the military balance in the Gulf. In August 1976, the United States and Iran agreed to a five-year arms deal worth about U.S. $3 billion. The U.S. Secretary of State defended the deal and argued that Iran needed a strong military presence to offset potential threats in its position bordering the Soviet Union for 1,250 miles. On August 7, *Pravda* accused the United States of using arms sales as a means of establishing American control over the Gulf to protect its oil interests. The *Pravda* attack followed the U.S. decision to sell Saudi Arabia 2,000 Sidewinder missiles and 400 Maverick tactical missiles for F-5 fighter planes that Saudi Arabia had already bought from the United States. When the Shah visited Moscow in 1974, Kosygin is reported to have asked him "Against whom will Iranian arms be used?" adding: "If it is against us, it is not enough." He is right; in terms of firepower there is no contest. But the geography of the Gulf and the availability of modern technology make it difficult to challenge a well-armed coastal state. Gulf waters can be defended by mines or blockades; these can be supported by shore-based missiles, long-range aircraft with stand-off missiles (such as the Condor and Harpoon), and fast patrol boats (FPB).

In short, if the Soviet fleet were to attempt to transit the Gulf during an emergency it would be extremely risky. Moreover, maritime straits may become territorial waters that would affect overflight and submerged passage. All the states are pro-Western in that there are common interests between producers and consumers. This is to the disadvantage of the Soviet Union, and any attempt to project its power will be too costly to either threaten or to implement (Amirie, 1976). Above all, the Western interest is directly served by Iran's colossal defense program; in particular Iran's navy dominates the Gulf. There is no serious competition, and by the mid-1980s Iran plans to be a major Indian Ocean naval power.

On the whole, superpower presence in the Indian Ocean has no significant impact on events in the Gulf, but this may soon change. New naval-weapon technologies have made oceans greater arenas for conflict; naval armament, fire control, maritime surveillance, antisubmarine warfare, and ship design have revived naval strategic planning. In this event, the regional states are fortunate in that the Gulf is a naval cul-de-sac; conversely, this is unattractive to the Soviet Union. From the northwest segment of the Indian Ocean, most of the western Soviet industrial areas and west Siberia are within the range of the U.S. Polaris missiles and of Poseidon MIRVs.

The Soviet Union has attempted to erode this nuclear disadvantage by deploying its own vessels in the Indian Ocean and by building military and naval installations in the Somali ports of Berbera, Mogadishu, and Kismayu. During 1976, the Soviet Union planned to bring into service up to 10 nuclear submarines—of which six will each carry 12-16 missiles with a range of 4,800 miles—and major surface ships, including a 40,000-ton aircraft carrier. On July 18, 1976, that carrier, the Kiev, passed through the Dardanelles on its maiden voyage. The Kiev's sister ship, the Minsk, which has been launched from the Black Sea shipyard in Nikolayev, will follow shortly. For the moment the combined afloat deployment of U.S., British, and French fleets in the Indian Ocean exceeds that of the Soviet Union. "Its naval power, while a growing and serious problem, is far weaker than combined allied naval strength in terms of tonnage, firepower, range, access to the sea, experience and seamanship" (Kissinger, 1976).

Nevertheless, it is more than a coincidence that Soviet naval power clearly corresponds to the oil tanker routes from the Gulf to Japan and the Western hemisphere. These routes convey 80 percent of NATO's oil supplies and 70 percent of the strategic materials of members of the alliance. This and other factors compelled Western contingency planners to look at an island strategy in the world's oceans. In December 1966, the United States and Britain began talks about the buildup of Diego Garcia in the Chagos archipelago in the Indian Ocean. At first all the littoral states strongly protested at the strategic purposes Diego Garcia was to serve. Yet by 1976, Soviet naval deployment in the Ocean and Soviet involvement in the Horn of Africa had become selfevident to some earlier skeptics. By mid-1976, Australia, a former opponent, agreed to increase air and naval surveillance in the Indian Ocean and possibly to take over some roles from the United States. Australia announced that it would increase its long-range maritime patrol force and would intensify joint naval and military exercises with the United States in the Indian Ocean. The Australian prime minister said that he was concerned about the extension of Russian activity in the area and the potential threat to the region's smaller nations (The Times, 1976). This concern was shared by the French government: in April, the Ministry of Marine in Paris announced that France would maintain a fleet of some 20 warships in the Indian Ocean indefinitely. The French navy's principal base in the Indian Ocean is the island of Reunion; "our forces in the Indian Ocean are not really connected with Djibouti; they are there to safeguard shipping such as tankers on the oil routes from the Persian Gulf" (Daily Telegraph, 1976). In this sense the security of the Gulf may depend to some extent on the SALT talks on naval arms limitation. But agreement on this issue threatens to be extremely difficult to achieve. In the past, Britain, the United States, the Soviet Union, and France had worked closely together on the assumption that the traditional freedom to roam the oceans should be maintained as far as possible. However, this view is now challenged by the fresh argument that while the new global Soviet fleet, being largely strait-bound, had a keen interest in maintaining the old freedoms, this was not necessarily the case for Western navies with much easier access to oceans. This is an argument presented by many nonaligned nations, some of which are Indian Ocean states. But this argument ignores the important interests that Western states have in assured access to the Gulf and the Malacca straits. The anti-Western opposition of littoral states, and domestic pressure in the West to prune defense budgets, create a potential balance of advantage favorable to the Russians. But even this fragile balance can be eroded; in April 1976, India and China agreed to resume diplomatic relations, and this must be seen as an undoubted setback to Soviet pretensions in the area. India's pro-Soviet disposition may weaken in response to China's weight in Asia and, indirectly, in the Indian Ocean.

If naval arms limitation talks are to get anywhere, they will depend on progress in other areas of détente. Given Western disenchantment with détente at the moment, there seems little advantage for the West in pursuing talks in naval limitation in the Indian Ocean. For the foreseeable future, the most that can be expected is agreement on access and zones of restraint. Some observers expressed fears that the opening of the Suez Canal in 1975 would enable Soviet warships to transit the Canal, thus saving the long journey from Vladivostok. But the strategic advantage is illusory because in the event of another Middle East war, if the Canal is not closed again, all shipping will immediately become hostage.

In the Gulf, all states claim free passage between the Indian Ocean and the Gulf; the interdependence of Iranian and Arab defense needs and Western—principally U.S.—commitments act as constraints on Soviet brinkmanship (Cottrell, 1975; Cottrell and Hahn, 1976). In this respect, Iran's naval program, which has numerous critics and problems, needs to be encouraged. During its buildup period to the mid-1980s Iran has discouraged a precipitate Western withdrawal from the Indian Ocean, so that Iranian diplomacy will be given the time to develop the sinews of a regional security arrangement.

V. GULF SECURITY

Since March 1975, Iran has periodically proposed some form of defense cooperation in the Gulf. During a visit to the United States in May that year, the Shah announced that "in the Persian Gulf we seek collective security." Two months later (July), Gulf foreign ministers met in Jeddah and endorsed, in principle, the idea of a defense summit. Six issues were examined:

(1) Limitations on foreign powers in the region;

(2) A guarantee of the territorial integrity of all states, presumably to nullify border disputes;

(3) A nonaggression pact among states;

(4) Mutual assistance against subversion and cooperation in military and intelligence affairs;

(5) Freedom of navigation; and

(6) Territorial divisions of the waters of the Gulf and limits of the continental shelf.

Since July 1975, the momentum of Gulf security talks has slowed. In 1976, the author was told by a Gulf ruler that national security must come first and that success at the local level would tend to create favorable conditions for wider regional initiatives. This is a sensible comment, because some of the states display maverick tendencies. In August 1976, Sheikh Zayed of Abu Dhabi and president of the UAE expressed his disappointment at the slow progress of federation. In an interview with a Bahrain newspaper he stated that he would refuse to accept another term as president when his first term ended in December 1976. He said he was dissatisfied with the attitude of his fellow rulers in tackling federal problems: "Would you believe that I have just spent a week among the Emirates trying to settle insignificant boundary disputes between them?" He added, "I will not continue as President. . . . the problem is the spirit with which my brother rulers are tackling the problems which face the federation." In July, the rulers were expected to approve a draft permanent constitution for the UAE, but they decided to extend the federation's present interim constitution by a further five years from December. The rulers differed over the sovereignty of individual emirates and the federal budget, of which Abu Dhabi pays more than 90 percent. In the interview, Sheikh Zayed said he was very distressed by the decision to extend the federation's transitional period:

If our people's hopes were disappointed once in this decision, I was disappointed a thousand times . . . I have struggled with all I have got to set up this federation and see it grow until it gained stature as a leading nation on the international and pan-Arab level. I feel now I have the right to rest and to allow my brothers and colleagues to continue the march [Financial Times, 1976].

This kind of disappointment could be serious, because Sheikh Zayed's record in promoting national and federal integration makes it desirable that he continue. It is a difficult task because it has taken five years (since 1971) for the UAE to reach its present stage of development, and Sheikh Zayed's understandable frustrations are echoed by skeptics who point to the wasteful proliferation in the development plans of the emirate: cement industries, a dry-dock, international airports, palaces, and a general profusion of prestige projects.

On the whole, current and prospective negotiations have a lot going for them: the Iran-Iraq accord of 1975 is still holding; Oman has won its counterinsurgency campaign; Iraq and Oman have resumed diplomatic relations, as have Saudi Arabia and the PDRY. In March and May 1976, King Khalid of Saudi Arabia, after a year of relative passivity, made his first tour of the Gulf since his accession in March 1975. All sides agreed that if a security pact is to succeed, there should be complete understanding between Iran, Iraq, and Saudi Arabia. But what still has to be worked out are the details: the form the pact would take, what the contribution of each state will be, how the bases will be distributed, whether there will be coordination on resources or arms, and whether the pact will take the form of a political as well as a military agreement.

All the Gulf states understand the desirability of some kind of security arrangement, but few rulers are prepared to sign any document that could be remotely binding. In any arrangement, a security pact would be the final accomplishment after bilateral and multilateral arrangements had been worked out. Yet there is a body of evidence suggesting that there are very few issues on which states could reach common agreement. One problem is an abstract one: in the search for a concept of security, the terminology and discipline are unfamiliar. In seeking areas of cooperation, the Gulf has problems similar to those of the European Community. One of the more unrealistic proposals was for the acquisition of nuclear energy; on other issues Gulf states have begun to pick at the edges. There has been some progress on pollution, conservation, fisheries, communication, and aviation. There has been much less progress on Gulf currency, information, and on an arms industry. Given the complexity of the problems and the lack of progress, there is a widespread view that bringing in all the states simultaneously coud have the same effect as too many cooks. Indicative of the lack of progress was the postponed security conference meeting of Gulf foreign ministers to have been held in June 1976 in Muscat. The ministers planned to meet again at the U.N. General Assembly in New York in September. As a result, some Arab states are reconsidering Iranian proposals that in turn have been modified to take account of the Arab view. These are simply to encourage bilateral deals on as many issues as possible, so as to create throughout the Gulf an intricate mesh of "linkages."

In the Gulf, talks on regional security are at an exploratory stage. Until 1971, all the worrying about security was done by the British; now the Gulf states are obliged to look to each other in a manner that could fulfill Dr. Kissinger's vision of local independent power.

REFÉRENCES

Agency for International Development (1975) Published in Washington, D.C.

Al Tali'a (1975) Published in Cairo (August).

AMIRIE, A. [ed.] (1976) The Persian Gulf and Indian Ocean in International Politics. Tehran: IIPES.

ANTHONY, J.D. (1975) Arab States of the Lower Gulf. Washington: Middle East Inst.

BILL, J.A. (1972) The Politics of Iran. Ohio: Merrill.

BUNDY, W.P. (1975) "Dictatorship and American foreign policy." Foreign Affairs (October).

Center for Mediterranean Studies (1972) The Changing Balance of Power in the Persian Gulf. Rome: Center for Med. Studies.

Chase Manhattan Bank, Energy Economics Division (1975) Capital Investments of the World Petroleum Industry.

CHUBIN, S. and S. ZABIH (1974) The Foreign Relations of Iran. Berkeley: Univ. of California Press.

COTTRELL, A.J. (1975) Iran: Diplomacy in a Regional and Global Context. Washington: Craftsman Press.

――― and W.F. HAHN (1976) Indian Ocean Naval Limitations. New York: National Strategy Inform. Center.

Daily Telegraph (1976, April 15) London, England.

Financial Times (1976, August 2) London, England.

HUREWITZ, J.C. (1974) The Persian Gulf. Foreign Policy Assn. Headline Series no. 220 (April).

KEDOURIE, E. (1974) Arabic Political Memoris. London: Frank Cass.

KELIDAR, A. (1975) Iraq: the Search for Stability. London: Inst. for the Study of Conflict.

KISSINGER, H. (1976) Inaugural Alastair Buchan Memorial Lecture, International Inst. of Strategic Studies (June 25).

――― (1975) Interview in Business Week (January 2).

MAULL, H. (1975) Oil and Influence. Adelphi Papers 117, International Inst. of Strategic Studies.

Middle East International (1976) "A security pact in the Gulf?" London (January).

NAKHLEH, E.A. (1975) Arab-American Relations in the Persian Gulf. Washington: American Enterprise Inst.

PRICE, D.L. (1975) Oman: Insurgency and Development. London: Inst. for the Study of Conflict.

Shah of Iran (1967) The White Revolution. Tehran: Imperial Pahlavi Library.

SMILEY, D. and P. KEMP (1975) Arabian Assignment. London: Cooper.

The Times (1976, August 10) London.